T0077963

HARDENING BY AUDITING

A Handbook for Measurably and
Immediately Improving the Security
Management of Any Organization

Eugene A. Razzetti

authorHOUSE®

AuthorHouse™
1663 Liberty Drive
Bloomington, IN 47403
www.authorhouse.com
Phone: 833-262-8899

Published by AuthorHouse 06/29/2022

ISBN: 978-1-6655-6260-7 (sc)
ISBN: 978-1-6655-6261-4 (e)

CONTENTS

SECTION I
INTERNAL AUDITING IN GENERAL

Section Two
Organizational Security Management

APPENDIX

DEDICATION

This is the second edition of my fourth book. I continue to dedicate it to my wonderful family – living and deceased, the United States Navy, where I learned first-hand about Ethics, Management, Security, and Accountability; and to YOU: the no nonsense management professional with a great deal to do and not much time to do it.

I hope that you will use it to "harden" the security of your organizations. The time is now.

FOREWORD

This book is an updated compendium of articles and checklists that I wrote on the subject of Organizational Security. It is based on work I have done as an auditor and management consultant in the U.S. and in Central America and as a Military Analyst for the Center for Naval Analyses, research of some very fine books, and the 27 years of Military Service that preceded it.

The premise of this book and my reason for creating it is simple:

1. *Our organizations (large and small – public and private) and, in fact, our lives are in danger from both physical and cyber-attacks, because we remain incredibly uneducated, unstructured, and vulnerable, when it comes to threats to our security.*

2. *Organizational Security can be upgraded profoundly through a well-developed program of internal and outside audits. This book stresses internal audits – those that you do by yourselves and within your walls.*

3. *Organizations can combine resources synergistically. That is, the whole of the effort will be greater than the sum of its parts.*

I have kept this work as compact as possible, so as to minimize reading time and maximize productivity. I write for no-nonsense CEOs, acquisition, security, and program managers in both the public and private sectors, with big responsibilities and limited resources. I refer often to four excellent ISO International Standards. They offer guidance for structuring effective management programs rapidly, regardless of whether or not organizations desire certification by accreditation bodies.

I invite you to use my approach to Risk Management, as explained in the pages that follow. You will find it an effective and uncomplicated method for developing and monitoring your strategic plans.

Checklists and "quick-looks" can bring you up to speed fast. Using the checklists provided and taking prompt, positive, action on your findings will improve your security posture almost immediately, as well as boost your confidence to take on greater challenges.

Good luck, and now let's get to work.
Gene Razzetti
Alexandria, VA

SECTION I

INTERNAL AUDITING
IN GENERAL

CHAPTER ONE

What We Mean by "Hardening by Auditing"

Ten areas in which executives and auditors can quantifiably improve the security posture of any organization.

Overview

Industrial espionage, hacker/cyber-attacks, natural disasters, disgruntled former employees, HAZMAT spills, and (let's face it) terrorist attacks can close an organization indefinitely, not to mention exacting a concurrent, incidental toll in personnel or equipment. Organizations, especially those contribute to the defense of the United States, have an ethical as well as an economic imperative to assess and *harden* their security structures. These days, Management can and should assess the security posture of their organizations as part of the organization's overall auditing strategy – no less vital than Quality, Finance, Marketing, or Human Resource Management.

The International Standard ISO 28000: Supply Chain Security Management can help to ensure the security of any organization. It was developed in response to the transportation and logistics industries' need for a commonly applicable security management system specific to the supply chain.

The main elements of the ISO 28000 Standard are:

✓ Security Management Policy
✓ Security Planning (risk assessment, regulatory requirements, objectives, and targets)

✓ Implementation and Operation (responsibilities and competence, communication, documentation, operational control, and emergency preparedness)
✓ Internal auditing, corrective and preventive Action
✓ Management review and continual improvement.

Organizations already certified to ISO 9000 Quality Management) or ISO 14000 (Environment Management) are already well on their way to ISO 28000 certification and to a hardened security posture. These three International Standards mutually support each other, as shown in the following table, and security-minded auditors and consultants will work with an organization's existing strategic planning, process management, and documentation, to synergistically increase security, as well as the more traditional challenges, like efficiency, safety, profitability, and regulatory compliance. See Table 1-1.

Table 1-1 Relationship of ISO Standards

Your Organization's Supply Chain	Quality ISO 9000	Environmental ISO 14000	Security ISO 28000
Procurement/ Purchasing	X	X	X
Manufacturing	X	X	X
Planning/Scheduling	X	X	X
Assembly	X	X	X
Processing General work flow	X	X	X
Warehousing/ Inventory	X	X	X
Transportation Distribution	X	X	X
Retailing	X	X	X
General modeling	X	X	X
Service	X	X	X

Ten areas in which executives and auditors can quantifiably harden the security of their organizations

The ten areas that follow contain segments of a checklist that I use when I audit or consult in ISO 28000. Appendix III contains my complete Supply Chain Security checklist.

1. Organizing the Security Management System

> *"Things refuse to be mismanaged long"*
> *Ralph Waldo Emerson*

Organizing for security means that the organization must establish, document, maintain, and continually improve an effective security management system for identifying security threats, assessing risks, and controlling/mitigating their consequences. The organization must look at all of the functions it performs and assess them according to the amount of vulnerability and the amount of protection required, as shown in the notional matrix below. Figure 1-1 describes a quick and logical vulnerability assessment. As the arrows suggest, you want to minimize vulnerability and maximize protection. Try this with your own organization and/or area of responsibility.

Figure 1-1 Vulnerability Assessment (example)

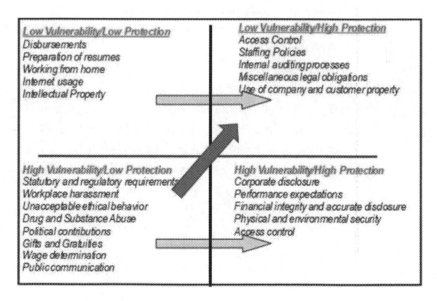

2. *Defining the Scope of the Security Management System*

Having completed an initial vulnerability assessment, the organization must next define the scope of its Security Management System, including control of outsourced processes that affect the conformity of product or service. That accomplished, the organization must establish (and maintain) an organizational structure, including roles, responsibilities, and authorities, consistent with the achievement of the security management policy, objectives, targets, and programs; and these must be defined, documented, and communicated to all responsible individuals.

Management must provide quantifiable and documented evidence of its commitment to development of a security management system and to improving its effectiveness. Specifically, by:

- Appointing a member of senior management who, irrespective of other responsibilities is responsible for the design, maintenance, documentation and improvement of the security management system
- Appointing members of management with the necessary authority to ensure that the objectives and targets are implemented
- Identifying and monitoring the expectations of the organization's stakeholders and taking appropriate action to manage these expectations[1]
- Ensuring the availability of adequate resources
- Communicating to the organization the importance of meeting its security management requirements in order to comply with its established policies
- Ensuring any security programs generated from other parts of the organization complement the security management system
- Communicating to the organization the importance of meeting its security management requirements in order to comply with its policy
- Establishing meaningful security metrics and measures of effectiveness, security-related threats, criticalities, and vulnerabilities are evaluated and included in organizational risk assessments as appropriate (see below)

---

[1] Please remember that "stakeholders" includes the surrounding community. Don't do anything that makes things worse for your neighbors.

3. Security Policies – taking a "security" approach to mission accomplishment

Top management also must develop, as applicable to the mission of the organization, written security policies that are:

- Consistent with the other policies of the organization
- Providing framework for specific security objectives, targets, and programs to be produced
- Consistent with the organization's overall security threat and risk management strategy
- Appropriate to the threats to the organization and the nature and scale of its operations
- Clear in their statement of overall/broad security management objectives
- Compliant with current applicable legislation, regulatory and statutory requirements and with other requirements to which the organization subscribes
- Visibly endorsed by top management
- Documented, implemented, and maintained
- Communicated to all relevant employees and third parties including contractors and visitors with the intent that these persons are made aware of their individual security-related obligations
- Available to stakeholders where appropriate
- Provided for review in case of acquisition or merger, or other change to the business scope, which may affect the relevance of the security management system.

4. Security Training and Qualification

The security-minded organization appoints (and entrusts) personnel to operate the Security Management System. Like any other responsible positions in the organization, the people who design, operate, and manage the security equipment and processes must be suitably *qualified* in terms of education, training, certification, and/or experience. Further, these personnel must be fully aware and supportive of:

5

a. The importance of compliance with security management policies and procedures, and to the requirements of the Security Management System as well as their roles and responsibilities in achieving compliance, including emergency preparedness and response; and

b. The potential consequences to the organization's security posture by departing from specified operating procedures.

5. *Operational Control*

A. General

Effective operational control of the Security Management System means that the organization has identified all operations necessary for achieving its stated security management policies, control of all activities, and mitigation of threats identified as posing significant risks. Control also means compliance with legal, statutory, and other regulatory security requirements, the security management objectives, delivery of its security management programs, and the required level of supply chain security (as appropriate).

ISO 28000 Certification requires organizations to ensure that operational control is maintained by:

- Establishing, implementing, and maintaining documented procedures to control situations where their absence could lead to failure to maintain operations
- Establishing and maintaining the requirements for goods or services which impact on security and communicating these to suppliers and contractors.

Where existing designs, installations, operations, etc., are changed, documentation of the changes should address attendant revisions to:

- Organizational structure, roles or responsibilities
- Security management policy, objectives, targets, or programs
- Processes or procedures.

Documenting the introduction of new security infrastructure, equipment, or technology, which may include hardware and/or software, should also include the introduction of new contractors or suppliers.

Almost every organization has some kind of supply chain, which, whether upstream or downstream of its activities, can have a profound influence on its operations, products, or services. Identifying, evaluating, and mitigating threats posed from upstream or downstream supply chain activities are as essential as performing the same functions inside your own fence line. The organization requires controls to mitigate potential security impacts to it and to other nodes in the supply chain as well.

B. Specific "Quick-looks"

Here are some immediate operational considerations for the forward-thinking and security-minded manager, trying to reduce the vulnerability and attractiveness of his organization or facility. Check these out by the end of the week:

- Intrusion detection systems
- Fences, security lighting, natural barriers
- CCTV
- Computer backup systems; firewalls
- Roof and ventilation duct accessibility
- Construction materials and thickness requirements
- Installed firefighting systems
- Roads and alleys
- Parking areas
- Locks, doors, and access control
- Identification management (i.e., employees, customers, vendors)
- Utilities (including uninterruptible power systems)
- Safes, desks, filing cabinets, controlled/exclusion areas
- HAZMAT generation and management
- Vehicle surveillance and security (including delivery and fuel trucks)
- Proximity of emergency services (e.g., fire, medical, police)
- Mail and package processing.

Table 1-2 A sample Quicklook checklist

Designation	Quick-look	Date	SAT/ UNSAT	Remarks
I-1	Intrusion Detection Systems			
I-2	Fences, Security lighting, natural barriers			
I-3	CCTV			
I-4	Computer backup systems; firewalls			
I-5	Roof and ventilator duct accessibility			
I-6	Construction materials/thickness requirements			
I-7	Roads and alleys			
I-8	Parking areas			
I-9	Locks, doors and access control			
I-10	Identification management			
I-11	Utilities (including uninterruptible power systems)			
I-12	Safes, desks, file cabinets. Controlled/exclusion areas			
I-13	Hazmat generation and management			
I-14	Vehicle surveillance/security			
I-15	Proximity of emergency services			
I-16	Mail and package processing			

Prepared/Date _____

Reviewed/Date_____

In Security as in fashion – go for the "layered" look.

6. Communication and Documentation

The organization must have procedures for ensuring that pertinent security management information is communicated to and from relevant employees, contractors, and stakeholders. This applies to outsourced operations as well as those taking place within the organization. This is especially important when dealing with sensitive or classified information.

Additionally, the organization must establish security management system documentation system that includes but is not limited to:

- The Security Management System scope, policy, objectives, and targets
- Description of the main components of the security management system and their interaction, and reference to related documents
- Documents including records determined by the organization to be necessary to ensure the effective planning, operation and control of processes that relate to its significant security threats and risks.

7. *Emergency Preparedness and Response*

Emergency response may be thought of as normal operations at faster-than-normal speeds, or it may mean something entirely different. The security-minded organization needs to establish, implement, and maintain appropriate plans and procedures (e.g., backing up of records or files) for responses to security incidents and emergency situations, and to prevent and/or mitigate the likely consequences associated with them. Emergency plans and procedures should include all information dealing with identified facilities or services that may be required during or after incidents or emergency situations, in order to maintain continuity of operations[2].

Organizations should periodically review the effectiveness of their emergency preparedness, response, and recovery plans and procedures, especially after the occurrence of incidents or emergency situations caused by security breaches and threats. Security-minded managers and auditors will test these procedures periodically (as applicable), including scheduling drills and exercises and developing corrective actions as appropriate.

8. *Auditing and Evaluation*

Periodic internal or outside security audits determine whether the organization is in compliance with relevant legislation and regulations, industry best practices, and conformance with its own policies and objectives. As with any other audit, organizations need to maintain records of results, findings, and required preventive and corrective action.

Security-minded organizations need to audit their security management plans, procedures, and capabilities. Security audits can include periodic reviews, testing, post-incident reports and lessons learned, performance evaluations, and exercises.

Significant findings and observations, once properly evaluated or gamed, should be reflected in revisions or modifications.

---

[2] The best emergency management plans that I have ever seen were for U.S. Naval Bases along the Gulf Coast, where the threat (and likelihood) of hurricanes is perennial and immense.

9. *Preventive and Corrective Action*

> **Audit ➡ Nonconformity ➡ P/C Action ➡ Corrected/Improved**

Good auditors discover nonconformities during audits. In doing so, they identify the need for either preventive or corrective action. Top management (hopefully) supports audit findings and initiates preventive or corrective actions as appropriate. There is no difference with *security* audits. In fact, the need for preventive and corrective action may be even more acute.

10. *Continual Improvement*

Continual improvement, the basis and underpinning of the ISO International Standards, must be thought of as an ongoing process and not an "end state". Top management must develop a continuous improvement *mindset* that says that we can always make something better. Continual improvement of organizational security requires top management to review the organization's security management system at planned intervals, in order to ensure its continuing suitability, adequacy, and effectiveness. Security audits and reviews should include assessing opportunities for improvement and the attendant need for changes to the security management system, including security policies and security objectives, plus threats and risks. Organizations already working with ISO 9000 and ISO 14000 can, with minimal effort, expand management reviews to cover security and well as quality and environmental management. A Security Management Review, either stand-alone or as part of other management reviews (e.g., ISO 9000), should include:

- Evaluations of compliance with legal and regulatory requirements and other requirements to which the organization subscribes
- Communication from external interested parties, including complaints
- The day-to-day security performance of the organization

- Facility or physical plant security (including motion sensors, firewalls, or perimeter fencing)
- The extent to which stated objectives and targets have been met
- The Security Risk Assessment strategy
- Status of corrective and preventive actions, and/or follow-up actions from previous management reviews
- Changing circumstances, including developments in legal and other requirements related to its security aspects
- Recommendations for improvement.

Outputs from security management reviews should include any decisions and actions changing the Security Management System, together with costs, schedules, and other justifications, and should be consistent with a mindset and commitment to continual improvement.

SUMMARY

Adding Organizational Security Management to your internal auditing schedule will harden your organization against the threats of today's world while also making it more competitive.

If you are already auditing your processes to an approved set of standards, or (better yet) International standards like ISO 9000 or ISO 14000, you are half-way there. If you are already auditing to ISO 28000, you *are* there. If the latter is the case, you already know what I am about to write. Organizations need to make security one of their missions, and then approach it like any other:

✓ Establish policies and procedures, conduct risk assessments,
✓ Implement processes
✓ Identify corrective actions
✓ Establish a mindset of continuous improvement
✓ And audit.

Organizations that cannot conduct their operations in a self-imposed and self-monitored secure environment may cease to exist just as certainly as organizations that cannot maintain operational effectiveness, profitability, or product or service superiority – only faster. They must *harden* their operations to protect them from either incidental or deliberate attack. Ongoing programs of internal security auditing are essential to the hardening process.

Top management must develop a continuous improvement mindset that says that we can always make something better.

CHAPTER TWO

Benchmarking, Dashboards, Metrics, and Measures of Effectiveness

Benchmarking

We can't discuss performance measurement in general or "dashboards" in particular without first discussing benchmarking. That is, determining and quantifying the *expected* performance from an operation or a process, in order to compare it to *actual* performance. Benchmarking identifies the *amount* of improvement possible. Once completed, an accurate benchmarking process allows Management to assess those operations or processes on a continuing basis, in order to identify areas for improvement. Figure 2-1 shows the relationship between expected and actual performance. The "gap" may be strategic, tactical, or operational, depending on the subject of the benchmarking process.[3]

Figure 2-1 Benchmarking and Gap Analysis

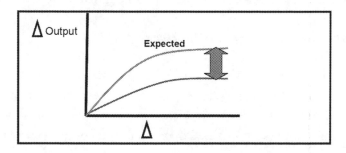

---

[3] Gap Analysis comes into play here, but that's a major study in itself.

Internal benchmarking examines an organization's own activities, those taking place inside its own walls. Areas always in need of internal benchmarking include (but are not limited to) facilities, manufacturing and material handling processes, administration, training, waste, work in progress, and reject rates.

External benchmarking can include customer satisfaction, competitors' products, recommendations from external consultants and auditors, public databases, and the annual reports of other companies.

1. *Benchmarking and Gap Analysis – Asking good questions and acting on the answers*

Benchmarking and gap analysis can be described as seeking out, identifying, and attempting to emulate and improve on established standards, contract requirements, or other best practices. Auditors use them to compare actual organizational performance with established standards.

Internal benchmarking examines activities taking place inside the organization's walls, such as manufacturing, training, waste, or work in progress. External benchmarking can include customer satisfaction (on-time delivery, reliability/defect reports, etc.) competitors' products, ISO 9000, ISO 14000, and other structured certification standards, as well as tradeshows, seminars, and workshops.

CEOs will not know the results of their decisions or changes without an effective benchmarking strategy. Internal audits can help determine how an organization is performing relative to how it should (i.e., the gap). Then, state the reasons for the gaps and the required corrective actions.

2. *Metrics and Measures of Effectiveness*

It has been said that what can't be measured can't be managed. CEOs must have the ability to subjectively and objectively quantify the success or failure of their operations, products, or services. They must be able to measure the components of those operations and compare their findings with established standards.

With the right mindset and the right metrics, CEOs and managers can perform the following:

- Optimally plan an entire throughput process, based on missions, load locations, and available resources
- Establish completion goals (pieces/day, number of days required, required deadlines)
- Evaluate operations in progress, and assess the ability of assigned resources to meet the established goals.

Once the optimal metrics and measures of effectiveness have been identified, CEOs and managers can employ them to assess all areas of operations, in order to meaningfully quantify:

- Decision making processes
- Intelligence collection
- Risk, vulnerability, and the allocation of limited resources
- Optimal reporting procedures
- Plotting and prediction procedures
- Alternative courses of action.

The CEO's Dashboard

As a military analyst, I spent some time developing training packages and spreadsheet models for potential port commanders in places like Kuwait, trying to establish metrics and measures of effectiveness that would resemble, as closely as possible, a "dashboard" for their operations. The goal was, obviously, to increase operational efficiency and minimize exposure to danger in terms of time spent and personnel required in dangerous places or situations. Dashboards provide drivers with vital information (e.g., fuel level, coolant temperature), immediate warning (e.g., red lights), and control (various dials and switches). Metrics and measures of effectiveness, often in the form of a spreadsheet model, provided those commanders with a dashboard equivalent.

As warfighters must have the ability to objectively measure the success or failure of their operations in a timely manner, so must CEOs and program managers be able to measure (or quantify) the potential profit or loss from intended operations or initiatives.

Metrics can be either *subjective* (i.e., conclusions based on observations, experience, and judgment) or *objective* (collected data). The tables that follow describe core subjective and objective metrics used to measure the potential effectiveness of business operations.

Subjective Metrics

Table 2-1 lists representative subjective metrics for quantifying the impact of operations or processes.

Table 2-1 Subjective metrics

Metric	Desired Movement/Change
Intelligence collection and dissemination accuracy	Increase
Risk/vulnerability	Decrease
Detection and reporting accuracy	Increase
Connectivity	Increase
Assessment of preparedness	Increase
Mission accomplishment	Increase
Maintenance of Situational Awareness	Increase
Accuracy of scanning and other electronic sensors	Increase
Weather prediction accuracy	Increase

Objective Metrics

Table 2-2 lists some representative objective metrics for quantifying operations or processes. These metrics are capable of quantification and not as susceptible to interpretation, license, or challenge as the subjective metrics in table 2-1.

Table 2-2 Objective metrics

Metric	Desired Movement/Change
Response Times (hours)	Decrease
Equipment downtime/time degraded (hours)	Decrease
Speed of movement (miles/hour)	Increase
Throughput (pieces/hour)	Increase
Situational Awareness/Common Operational Picture (square miles)	Increase
Commonality/Interoperability (instances)	Increase
Unit Costs (dollars)	Decrease
Delivery times (hours)	Decrease
Required training time (hours)	Decrease
Route distances (miles)	Decrease
Decontamination time (hours)	Decrease
Personnel casualties (personnel)	Decrease
Extent of operational disruption (days/hours)	Decrease

The development and promulgation of goals and objectives, as described earlier, are essential for an organization's ultimate success, and the ultimate success of the goals and objectives depends on the appropriateness and comprehensiveness of the metrics and measures of effectiveness with which they are measured.

Metrics and measures of effectiveness, usually in the form of a spreadsheet model, provided those commanders with a dashboard equivalent.

As warfighters must have the ability to objectively measure the success or failure of their operations in a timely manner, so must CEOs and program managers be able to measure (or quantify) the potential profit or loss from intended operations or initiatives.

Decision makers, both Military and civilian, need to apply metrics and measures of effectiveness to all areas of their operations, to meaningfully quantify:

- Information collection and dissemination
- Risk, vulnerability, and the allocation of limited resources[4]
- Optimal data collection and reporting procedures
- Implementation status of goals and objectives
- Alternative courses of action
- Situational awareness (internal and external).

Metrics can be either *subjective* (i.e., conclusions based on observations, experience, and judgment) or *objective* (used on collected data). The tables that follow describe core subjective and objective metrics used to measure the potential effectiveness of business operations.

3. Key Performance Indicators

The following is a selection of "key performance indicators". That is, measurable, replicable, and "audit-able" metrics that Management can use to continuously assess its performance. Some number of these will be applicable to your operations. Remember: you can measure almost anything.

a. Operational metrics

- ☐ Throughput
- ☐ Throughput as a percent of capacity
- ☐ Defects as a percent of throughput
- ☐ Number of order deliveries past due
- ☐ Rush order percent
- ☐ On-time delivery percent
- ☐ Customer satisfaction rating
- ☐ Number of complaints
- ☐ Number of complaints to revenue

---

[4] See Risk Management in the next chapter.

- [ ] Returns as a percent of units delivered
- [ ] Number of manual journal vouchers/entries per employee
- [ ] Ration of support staff to number of employees
- [ ] Days of inventory outstanding
- [ ] Inventory turns
- [ ] Market share
- [ ] Number of outstanding audit issues
- [ ] Book to bill ratio
- [ ] Day's sales outstanding
- [ ] Overtime percent
- [ ] Days without workplace injury
- [ ] Number of hours that production is off-line
- [ ] Personnel/material requisitions open past threshold or benchmark

b. Exception Reporting

- [ ] Audit reports
- [ ] Assets assigned to employees in excess of threshold or benchmark
- [ ] Unauthorized system access attempts
- [ ] General ledger accounts without assigned owners
- [ ] Assets without assigned owners
- [ ] Un-reconciled accounts
- [ ] Inventory aged over threshold
- [ ] Wires/checks issued over $ threshold
- [ ] Deliveries overdue/past-due over threshold
- [ ] Sales to unapproved customers
- [ ] Sales to customers over established limits
- [ ] Was or suspense accounts (or other accounts that should have a zero balance) that still have a balance
- [ ] Unavailable materials report
- [ ] Inventory count differences
- [ ] Purchase orders aged over threshold
- [ ] Unmatched receipts
- [ ] Unsigned management representation of financial results

c. Financial Metrics

- ☐ Cost per unit
- ☐ Revenue per full time equivalent
- ☐ Employee expenses headcount
- ☐ Accounts receivable turnover
- ☐ Write-offs as a percent of sales
- ☐ Reserves as a percent of assets
- ☐ Reserves as a percent of accounts receivable over 90 days past due
- ☐ Budget to actual variances
- ☐ Value at risk
- ☐ Market value to contract value of financial interests
- ☐ Un-reconciled accounts exposure
- ☐ Accounts payable aging
- ☐ Financial costs as a percent of revenue
- ☐ Margin percent
- ☐ Regulatory capital charges
- ☐ Working capital
- ☐ Interest coverage
- ☐ Sales, general and administrative expenses as a percent of revenue
- ☐ Earnings per share
- ☐ Risk-adjusted return on capital
- ☐ Debt/equity trend

d. Monitoring

- ☐ Internal threat analysis of competitor-controlled incidents
- ☐ Evaluation of proposed or pending legislation effects on current operations
- ☐ Periodic threat analysis of extremist groups on current operations
- ☐ Camera surveillance of key areas to identify illegal activity.

4. *Turning recurring reports into management tools.*

An admiral I once served under told his staff that a *new reporting requirement could not be imposed without removing an existing reporting requirement.* That helped to limit the *quantity* of reports required by operating forces (who had better things to do). Next, he tasked staff members to find redundant reporting requirements and eliminate or consolidate them. (Good job, Boss!)

The next challenge should have been to determine what useful information the reports actually contained, and whether anybody really needed it. We never addressed the "quality" or "usefulness" of the reports, only the "quantity" and "frequency".

Reports cannot be useful management tools unless they can measurably, credibly, and defensibly, contribute to:

- Making decisions
- Information collection and management
- Risk and vulnerability analysis, and the allocation of limited resources
- Plotting and prediction procedures
- Planning alternative courses of action.

In other words, the reports and the preparation that they require should "add value" to the organization and its processes.

"Value-add" reporting should also:

- Include recommended preventive or corrective action
- Contain important information, reflecting a genuine need, and containing measurable assessment and analyses for decision making.
- Determine whether separate but similar reports are being sent to different organizations, and (if so) create a single report covering multiple submission requirements.
- Contain built-in, follow-up mechanisms complete with responsibilities assigned and projected milestones or completion dates.

A "value-add" report can thus become a plan of action, totally in keeping with an organization's strategic planning, risk management, and budgeting and competitive strategies.

SUMMARY

The metrics and measures of effectiveness used in decision making must, like a car's dashboard, deliver credible, useful, information, almost as immediately. Audits often confirm that decision making models are in place and being used. However, audits, can also confirm not only the existence of the models but also their strategic applicability. That is, their currency, accuracy, and usefulness, as well as the data and logic from which they were developed.

With the right mindset and the right metrics, CEOs and managers can:

- Optimally plan entire processes, based on missions, load locations, and available resources
- Establish completion goals (pieces/day, number of days required, required deadlines)
- Monitor and evaluate operations in progress, and assess the ability of assigned resources to meet the established goals and objectives.

CHAPTER THREE

Defense Contracting

Toward a Performance (and Quality)-Based Adaptive Acquisition Framework – AAF meets ISO

Ten ways to get off to the right start

The two primary directives of the Adaptive Acquisition Framework (AAF) are (1) DoDD 5000.01 The Defense Acquisition System (DAS); and (2) DoDI 5000.02: Operation of the Adaptive Acquisition Framework. Both are comprehensive, prescriptive, vague, and ponderous.

The DoD directives provide well-meaning but weighty guidance about "what to do," but little useful assistance regarding "*how* to do it" (or even how do you know when you *have* done it), leaving it to program managers; and word search of the following terms: "quality", "audit", "verification", and "validation" will get you: *"No matches were found"* for both directives.

This chapter concerns the pertinency and utility of the ISO International Standards alongside the requirements of the AAF. It, I hope to convince readers in general and program managers in particular to use The International Standards Organization (ISO) management standards. These are tried, tested, and ready-to-go standards, that provide structure and direction for both the creation and execution of Defense acquisition contracts – fulfilling (and clarifying) AAF requirements.

In the past, I have written about and stressed the need for the following competencies in management of DoD programs:

- Risk management and gap analysis
- Operator and/or warfighter participation
- Meaningful feedback, follow-up, and accountability
- Modeling and simulation, including tabletop exercises and/or wargames
- Contingency and continuity planning
- Working through and after a pandemic
- Second party auditing.

These competencies (and *mindsets*) are endemic to the ISO programs and where AAF can meet ISO.

> *A credible, no-nonsense, working document and indispensable management tool should replace an often contrived and superficial work of "semi-fiction."*

When ISO 9001:1994 (the first iteration, already positively received in Europe and Asia) was introduced inside the Beltway, the strategy was that ISO 9000-Certified contractors could simply submit copies of their (already existing) quality manuals in response to requests for proposal (RFP) – foregoing forever the need for creating those great tomes of questionable veracity known as *proposals*. Requests for proposals <u>ask</u> the question: "How would you solve *my* problem if you get the contract?" Quality manuals pre-emptively <u>answer</u> the question: "What service are you *already providing for all your clients?*"

Quality manuals (and/or operating procedures (OPs)) developed in accordance with ISO 9000 (for example) must meet, initially and periodically, the certification requirements of the ISO Standard, as evaluated by an accredited certification body, called an ISO Registrar. An ISO-certified quality manual would be a welcomed replacement for a proposal.

Think of it: A credible, no-nonsense, and indispensable management tool would replace an often contrived, superficial, and self-serving work of semi-fiction. And all those PowerPoint and "cut-and-paste" engineers could channel their efforts more productively.

In consulting circles, it's said that writing a proposal to address specifically all DoD contract requirements credibly is like trying to invent the "self-licking iced cream cone."

> *ISO certification requires nothing more than a responsible DoD contractor should be doing already; and nothing more than a DoD Program Manager should expect.*

Table 3-1 summarizes the readiness of four of the major ISO International Standards to address the stated operating policies of the AAF. The relationship is summarized in figure 3-1.

Table 3-1 Addressing AAF requirements with the ISO Standards

Nr	AAF Operating Policies (Ref: DoDI 5000.02)	ISO 9000 Quality Management System Clauses *	Applicable ISO Standard
1.	Simplify Acquisition Policy	Quality policies, goals, & objectives; Risk-based thinking; environmental aspects; Implementation & operation; Continual improvement; Product/process development	1,2,3,4
2.	Tailor Acquisition Approaches	Quality, policies, goals, & objectives; Operational planning & control; Design & development controls	1,2,3,4
3.	Empower Program Managers	Quality policies, goals, & objectives; Management review; Internal audit; checklist development; Communication Feedback, follow-up, & accountability;	1,2,3,4
4.	Conduct Data-driven Analysis	Quality policies, goals, & objectives; Information systems and Supply chain security management targets, data analysis & evaluation; Performance evaluation; Control of changes; Measurement and traceability	1,2,3,4
5.	Actively Manage Risk	Risk-based thinking; Quality policies, goals, & objectives; Threats, criticalities, & vulnerabilities; Establish acceptable/unacceptable risk parameters; Control of nonconforming product	1,2,3,4
6.	Emphasize Sustainment	Quality policies, goals, & objectives; Implementation & operation; Continual improvement; Nonconformity & corrective action; Preservation	1,2,3,4

ISO Standards
1. ISO 9000: Quality Management Systems
2. ISO 14000: Environmental Management Systems
3. ISO 27000: Information Security Management Systems
4. ISO 28000: Supply Chain Security Management Systems

* Note: The other three Standards have similar clauses

ISO certification requires no more than what a responsible DoD contractor should be doing anyway- and what a responsible DoD program manager should expect.

Figure 3-1 The relationship of AAF and ISO

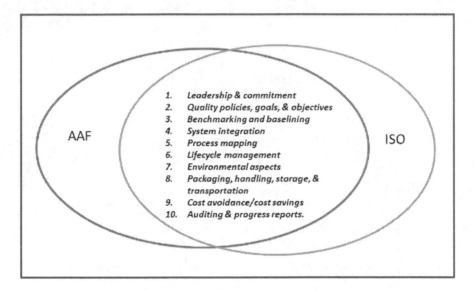

The sections that follow cover ten specific competencies necessary for successful management of DoD programs in accordance with both ISO and AAF, and in amplification of table 1; and how the ISO Standards (and an ISO mindset) can help to ensure the success of those programs.

1. Leadership and commitment

DoD directives require product support managers to "develop, plan, and implement a comprehensive product support strategy for all integrated product support elements and their material readiness." ISO 9001:2015 Clause 5.1 (for example) walks managers through (to name a few):

- Accountability;
- Allocation of resources;
- Roles, responsibilities, and authorities;

- Establishing policies, goals, and objectives; and
- Continual improvement.

You already know what you need to know about leadership and commitment. There is nothing new or different in the ISO Standards – just more accommodation and support.

2. Quality policies, goals, and objectives

Decision makers, both Military and civilian, need to establish goals and objectives for all areas of their programs, to meaningfully quantify:

- Information collection and dissemination;
- Risk, vulnerability, and the allocation of limited resources;
- Optimal data collection and reporting procedures;
- Implementation status of goals and objectives;
- Alternative courses of action; and
- Situational awareness (internal and external).

Figures 3-2 and 3-3 describe development and auditing of goals and objectives as part of the DoD acquisition big picture.

Figure 3-2 Transitioning an organization's vision into measurable goals and objectives.

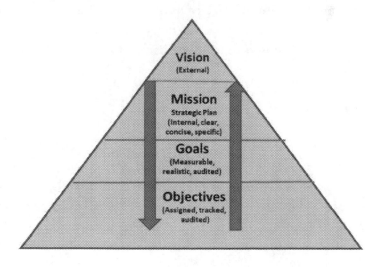

Figure 3-3 Auditing goals and objectives in the big picture

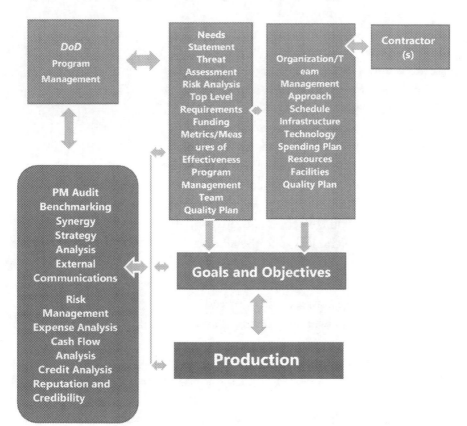

Metrics and measures of effectiveness are vital, and the metrics used to assess the effectiveness of the program can be either *subjective* (i.e., conclusions based on observations, experience, and judgment) or *objective* (based on collected data).

3.   Due diligence – just "due" it

Due diligence means, essentially, to make sure that all the facts regarding an organization are available and have been independently verified. Often, in major organizations, designated due diligence "teams" consisting of financial, technical, and/or legal experts, review and analyze all operative documents and assess top management's effectiveness. I know of no such effort with DoD contracts, but strongly suggest that it be considered. In the absence of that, program managers can assess (on their own) many due diligence processes vital to contract success, to include:

- *Environmental* due diligence during commercial real estate transactions can include environmental site assessments to avoid liability under the Comprehensive Environmental Response, Compensation, and Liability Act (CERCLA), commonly referred to as the "Superfund law".
- *Manufacturing* due diligence contains a number of concepts involving either the performance of source inspections or surveillances, the performance of quality duties such as Process Validation Assessment (PVA), or system audits with a certain standard of performance.
- Due diligence in *supplier quality* is the effort made by safety, quality and environmental professionals to validate conformance of products provided by sellers to purchasers. Failure to make this effort may be considered negligence.
- *Investigative* due diligence involves a general obligation to identify true root causes for non-compliance to meet a standard or contract requirement.

The ISO Standards do not refer specifically to Due Diligence, but do provide guidance in clauses such as ISO 9001:2015 Clause 8.4: *Control of externally provided processes, products, and services.* An ISO 9000-certified contractor should be ready to provide documented, audited, proof of compliance with this clause and adherence to the many-faceted areas of due diligence.

4. *System integration and connectivity*

System Integration is the process of bringing together component sub-systems into one system. It is an aggregation of sub-systems cooperating so that the resultant system is able to deliver an overarching functionality or capability by ensuring that the subsystems function together as *one* system. In information technology, this is the process of linking together different computing systems and software applications physically or functionally, to act as a coordinated whole. An integrated system streamlines processes, reduces costs and increases efficiency.

The current version of ISO 9000 (ISO 9001:2015) Clause 8.5: *Production and service provision* refers to product/service characteristics, results to be achieved, infrastructure, and measures of effectiveness.

Figure 3-4 describes system integration and connectivity.

Figure 3-4 System integration and connectivity

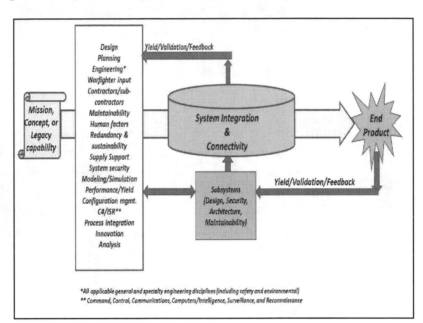

The current versions of ISO 27000 and ISO 28000 (especially) address virtually every competency described in figure 13-4, but from a *management* perspective, so program managers are not lost in the weeds. See the legend with Table 3-1.

5. *Process mapping*

Process maps, also called "process flow charts", or (if you're old like me) "flow process charts" are graphical representations to help visualize the details of key processes and support decision making. One can identify the major areas of strengths, weaknesses, and critical paths in existing processes; and the contribution of each individual step in the process. Process maps can spotlight cycle times, redundancies, and defects.

The major components of a process map include the inputs, outputs, and the steps in the process. A good process map should illustrate the flow of the work and the interaction with the organization. It should use common language/symbols that are easily understood. An ideal process map should contain proper detail with respect to multiple paths, decisions and rework loops.

Over the years, straightforward process maps have replaced wordy quality manuals and operating procedures in the implementation of ISO-compatible processes. Figure 13-5 is an ISO-compatible process map. A comprehensive process map can replace wordy quality procedure.

Figure 3-5 A general purpose process map

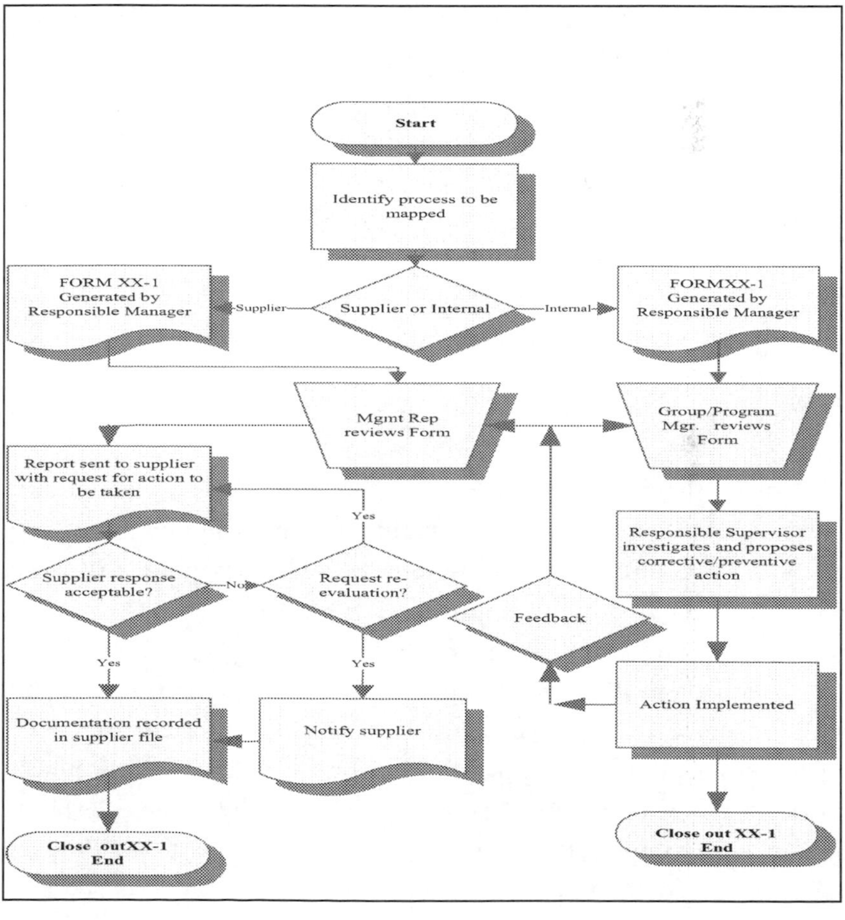

Process maps assure a contractor's understanding of the work to be done. It is virtually impossible to produce a correct process map without totally screening and understanding the process. Program managers would find it much more productive to review a contractor's process maps than his/her proposal. Process maps posted at work stations help to assure continuing adherence to specified requirements throughout the product development process. Internal auditing of the process(es) is streamlined as well.

6. Lifecycle (cradle to grave) management

Product Lifecycle Management or "PLM" means managing the entire lifecycle of a product from inception, through engineering design and manufacture, to service and disposal of manufactured products in accordance with environmental requirements. DoD program managers' responsibilities don't end with the delivery of a final product (e.g.; ship or weapons system). They must plan beyond product "use" and up to and including the proper disposal of whatever is left.

Since its initial publication in 1996, ISO 14000: Environmental Management Systems, has guided forward-thinking companies though product lifecycles, and, in doing so, has taken them beyond rote environmental *compliance* and into sound environmental *management*.

7. Environmental aspects

"Environment" means the surroundings in which an organization operates, including air, water, land, natural resources, terrain, flora, fauna, and humans – individually, as communities, and as part of a global system. Every organization, public or private, large or small, needs to practice pollution prevention and energy conservation.

An environmental "aspect" is an element of an organization's activities, products, or services, with the potential to impact on the environment. A significant environmental aspect has or can have a significant environmental impact (e.g., the creation of hazardous waste as a byproduct). A process byproduct that impacts the environment, such as sandblast grit, lead-based paint, or waste oil, can stop work at that facility for an indefinite period of time and result in potential legal action against the contractor – regardless of how critical the end-product may be to the Warfighter.

Taking aboard the lessons of lifecycle management, the program manager's "cradle to grave" approach, is not just with the product itself but with the environmental aspects that surround it throughout.

ISO 14000 takes the program manager calmly but deliberately through a robust environmental management program; and, as we auditors say: "If you think having an environmental management program is expensive – try *not* having one."

8. *Packaging, Handling, Storage, and Transportation*

Packaging, Handling, Storage and Transportation (PHS&T) is an essential subset of DoD acquisition and logistics planning, dealing with not only the timely arrival of products to warfighters, but minimizing the risk of damage, deterioration, or corrosion enroute – even for products destined for remote, austere, and environmentally unfriendly staging areas in-theater (e.g.; the Middle East).

Robust PHS&T requirements procedures established early in product development phases promote cradle-to-grave supportability and sustainability of major end items, reparable system elements and supporting test equipment, while minimizing the impact on the environment.

Product design and development in accordance with ISO 9001:2015 Clause 8.3: *Design and development of products and services* can optimize PHS&T practices.

9. *Cost avoidance and cost savings*

Cost avoidance focuses on actions to avoid incurring costs *in the future*. In business, this means taking measures to lower potential increased expenses so that a company doesn't have as many costs in the future. With cost avoidance, all actions are taken to reduce future costs.

Cost *savings*, also referred to as "hard savings," means any action that lowers *current* spending, investment, or debt levels.

ISO 9001:2015: Clause 9.1.3: *Analysis and evaluation* and 9.2: *Internal Audit* can walk program management through cost avoidance and cost savings issues as part of a product's overall performance effectiveness.

10. Auditing and progress reports

With the contract signed, the workers hired, the bonuses paid, and the empty champagne bottles removed from the conference room, DoD program managers often ask themselves: "What happens now?" "Is it done" and "have I lost my hammer?"

No. If you planned well, you should have a meaningful structure of periodic reports, allowing you to manage your program through its life.

Documentation produced in accordance with ISO Standards inevitably result in reduction of effort, volume, and redundancy. More importantly, the documentation becomes more "purposeful." "Monthly progress reports" become valuable *management tools*; as meaningless bulk and administrivia are replaced with trends, graphs, analyses, projections, and predictions; and updated EXCEL spreadsheets replace re-written, formatted, narratives – replete with dated metrics and purposes.

Assessing the readiness of a contractor to undertake a DoD contract should include assessing the ability of that contractor to effectively audit itself, and to submit to the auditing of outside registrars.

SUMMARY

Proposals often promise a happy future by touching all the bases on the RFP. RFPs in turn reflect the vague requirements of the AAF. This could be considered "where the clouds meet the tea leaves."

Vague and/or ponderous guidance is worse than no guidance at all. ISO certification requires no more than that which a responsible DoD contractor should be doing anyway; and no more than that which a responsible DoD program manager should expect. Certification to one or more of the major ISO International Standards, as attested to by an authorized accreditation body, can (and should) replace writing and submitting proposals. Quality manuals are real; what the contractor is doing now. They predict the future by realistically and convincingly describing the present.

My recommendation remains that DoD program managers download and learn the four major ISO International Standards shown in table 13-1, insist upon certification by aspiring contractors, and adapt DoD program management accordingly; and within the requirements of the AAF.

CHAPTER FOUR

Risk Management

> *I refer to risk management as "disciplined subjectivity" because you subjectively assess your threats, criticalities, and vulnerabilities by using your knowledge and experience. But you bring discipline to the work by assigning them a consistent, replicable, set of numerical values or "criteria". You cannot do risk management just by assessing risks in your head, or by yourself. I have developed straight-forward risk management processes like the process identified below for both Military and civilian applications. Try it and contact me if you have any questions. You'll like it.*

The terms *risk analysis, risk assessment,* and *risk management,* often used interchangeably, can mean a variety of different concepts and/or metrics. In point of fact, there is no one single approach to risk management. Approaches and strategies can be as simple or complex as Security Risk Assessment is the foundation of an organization's emergency management program. A properly conducted security risk assessment allows decisions to be made based on realistic scenario assumptions and provides justification for commitment of program resources.

the processes they were made to assess. However, simpler is almost always better, and using a spreadsheet that automatically computes and displays the assessments is better still.

Doing risk management on a spreadsheet customized for your organization can provide you with a fast, descriptive tool to:

- Standardize, assess, prioritize, and display readiness for specific business or mission scenarios
- Predict the impact of personnel and material changes before time or funds are expended
- Create uniform reports to higher authority
- Predict readiness by assessing risks.

Functions (e.g., sums, multiplications, averages) can be programmed into the spreadsheet, and graphs can be created automatically as values are introduced or changed, as will be shown.

This chapter develops a risk management program for your organization that:

- Identifies the threats (i.e., hazards or adverse events) to the organization
- Predicts the probability of the threat occurring
- Predicts the consequences of the threat occurring.[5]

Then, (and unlike more basic risk prediction models):

- Predicts the impact of one or more external or environmental factors; and finally:
- Predicts the change if a selected course of action (COA) is implemented.[6]

Creating risk assessment criteria

For assessments to be consistent, and reports to be uniform among reporting departments, and for the management tool we are creating to help in the decision-making process, we need standard numerical values or "criteria" to assess:

Threats to the mission or operation

Vulnerability of the mission or process to threats

Criticality of the process to the overall mission of the organization.

---

[5] We refer to this as computing basic risk assessment.

[6] This is advanced risk assessment, leading the way to meaningful risk *management*.

A basic EXCEL spreadsheet model, consisting of a set of connected worksheets, can be a priceless management tool for the CEO, because it forces him/her to:

- Identify the major potential <u>threats</u> to the mission of the organization
- Prioritize them, by assigning a numerical value to each (to be explained later)
- Evaluate the <u>criticality</u> of the part of the mission potentially impacted by the threat in terms of a numerical value
- Evaluate the <u>vulnerability</u> of the mission or organization to impact by the threat in terms of a numerical value.

Table 3-1 contains a notional set of numerical values from 1 to 10 and defines each in terms of threat, criticality, and vulnerability. These are the numbers we will use to complete the risk assessment process.

Table 4-1 The Criteria Table

Level	Scale	Threat Criteria	Criticality Criteria	Vulnerability Criteria
Lowest	1,2	Never occurred before - unlikely; minimally effective due to physical area/ environment; not a significant source of disruption	Minimally disruptive to mission if used	Minimally vulnerable to attack, due to own tactics, equipment, physical surroundings
Low	3,4	Has occurred before - possible; effective in physical area for short period; potential source of disruption	Disruptive to mission if used; minor mission degradation	Susceptible to attack, but history and physical surroundings make attack unlikely
Medium	5,6	Occurs periodically and predictably; likely to encounter; disruptive when occurring	Mission degraded, but can continue if attacked; some casualties	Highly vulnerable to attack, due to own tactical limitations and physical surroundings
High	7,8	Occurs often; enemy has expertise; utility in area against missions, expect to encounter; highly disruptive	Mission seriously degraded, but can continue marginally if attacked; significant casualties possible	Extremely vulnerable due to tactical and equipment limitations and physical surroundings
Highest	9,10	High probability of use; enemy proficient in use; unlimited utility and effectiveness against most missions; catastrophic if used	Mission failure; much disruption likely	Imminent danger, due to nature of operations, plus equipment limitations

The Threat Assessment Spreadsheet

Table 4-2 is an example of a threat assessment matrix or threat assessment spreadsheet. The notional missions or processes of the organization are listed on the vertical axis and the potential threats along the horizontal axis. Once you have identified both, it remains only to assign subjective numerical values from the Criteria Table.

Our spreadsheets contain normally expected organizational processes and eight notional threats to those processes. Risk managers, having identified the threats, assign numbers from the Criteria Table, based on their knowledge and experience. The spreadsheet automatically computes the total and the average threat[7]. We use the average threat in all the subsequent calculations. Some users use the highest threat figure in the row instead of the average threat figure. That's OK, as long as they use it consistently throughout the risk assessment process. The user may want to modify any or all of these matrices and calculations to suit his/her own preferences. Some modifications may prove misleading or self-defeating (such as using "0"). You will find them out soon enough. It is only important to be *consistent* throughout the process.

Table 4-2 Sample threat assessment matrix

Organizational Tasks	Terrorist Attack	Utility Loss	Hacker/Cyber Attack	Industrial Espionage	Strike	Agent Spill	Natural Disaster	Falsified reporting	Total	Average
Product Design	9	4	9	9	3	5	8	8	55	7
Product Development	4	4	9	9	3	5	8	8	50	6
Manufacturing	9	9	9	5	3	5	8	8	56	7
Measurement & Testing	9	4	9	5	6	5	8	8	54	7
Internal Movement	9	4	6	5	6	5	8	8	51	6
Warehousing	6	4	6	5	3	5	8	8	45	6
Marketing	4	4	6	5	3	5	8	8	43	5
Accounting	4	4	7	5	3	5	8	8	44	6
Planning	4	4	8	5	3	5	8	8	45	6
Shipping	9	4	6	5	6	5	8	8	51	6
Receiving	5	4	6	5	6	5	8	8	47	6
Misc. Clerical	4	4	7	5	3	5	8	8	44	6
Order Processing	6	4	4	7	6	5	8	8	48	6
Customer Sales & Service	4	4	6	5	6	5	8	8	46	6
Document Retrieval	8	4	6	5	3	5	8	8	47	6
Command & Control	4	4	6	8	3	5	8	8	46	6
Data Analysis	7	4	6	8	3	5	8	8	49	6
General Management	7	4	6	5	6	5	8	8	49	6

---

[7] This is the simplest way I have found to do this. You may have another way. You must, however, be consistent in whatever method you develop.

The model uses the "Average" threat values, which automatically post to the risk assessment spreadsheet.[8]

Computing Unadjusted Risk

As the planners complete the threat spreadsheet they identify and assess the threats to the organization. The next spreadsheet automatically copies the computed average threat for each organizational task and allows us to compute unadjusted (i.e., basic) risk according to the formula:

Risk = Criticality x Vulnerability x Threat

To determine unadjusted risk, the planner now assigns numerical values from the (same) Criteria Table for:

- The *criticality* of the threat incident or adverse event (if it happened) to the specific organizational task; and
- The *vulnerability* of the organization to the threat incident or adverse event.

How *vulnerable* the organization may be is a function of what actions it either must take or has already taken to mitigate or preclude the threat or event. For example, posting extra security personnel or adding alarm systems decreases an organization's *vulnerability* to a break-in. The alarm systems have not decreased the threat of a break-in, or the criticality of a break-in; only the vulnerability. Accordingly, you reduce risk by reducing vulnerability. Realizing this is essential for the CEO and risk manager. Table 4-3 computes basic risk assessment. This is often the final step in risk *assessment,* but it is only the beginning of risk *management,* as you will see. [9]

---

[8] The shaded columns are posted or computed automatically by the software.
[9] The shaded columns are posted or computed automatically, and the numbers are rounded off. You don't have to do anything with them.

Table 4-3 Computing basic risk

Organizational Tasks	Criticality	Vulnerability	Threat	Risk
Product Design	8	6	7	330
Product Development	8	5	6	250
Manufacturing	8	5	7	280
Measurement & Testing	8	4	7	216
Internal Movement	5	5	6	159
Warehousing	7	6	6	236
Marketing	4	7	5	151
Accounting	5	6	6	165
Planning	8	5	6	225
Shipping	5	4	6	128
Receiving	4	7	6	165
Misc. Clerical	4	5	6	110
Order Processing	4	5	6	120
Customer Sales & Service	7	6	6	242
Document Retrieval	8	6	6	282
Command & Control	4	6	6	138
Data Analysis	5	6	6	184
General Management	5	6	6	184

Advanced risk assessment calculation #1: Assessing the impact of the external environment

Risk = Criticality x Vulnerability x Threat x Environmental Adjustment

I originally added this step to the modeling process to assess the impact of host nation support on military logistic operations overseas. In some cases, host nation support/ involvement was invaluable, as with assignment of interpreters or counterparts. In other cases, (e.g., corrupt bureaucracies), U.S. forces were often better left alone. Organizations wanting to separately reflect this often-critical variable can add this step to assess:

- Foreign country support (receipt, transportation, customs, etc.)
- Supply chain security
- Outsourcing (foreign or domestic)
- Special laws, regulations, or protocols
- Anything else you want to separate from the internal processes but you feel must be included in the overall risk assessment process.

To show the impact of the external factors (whatever you decide to call them), multiply the computed basic risk by the number determined from table 3-4.

Table 4-4 Representative external environment numerical values and narrative descriptions

Scale	Criteria
0.1 - 0.5	Invaluable support - enhanced mission conduct and efficiency 0.6 - 0.9 Effective - minimal mission support
0.6-0.9	Effective - minimal mission support
1.0	No significant support or degradation
1.1 – 1.4	Degradation of mission, making accomplishment difficult to very difficult, with increasingly greater mission vulnerability; mission less safe/less efficient
1.5 – 2.0	Severe degradation with possible to likely mission failure

For example, if the addition of a certain procedure or custom in the country where your process is outsourced decreases the risk by half, you multiply the risk figure by .5. If the practice makes no appreciable difference, multiply the risk by 1 (no change). If a procedure makes it half again as difficult or risky, multiply by 1.5. Again, this will not corrupt or hinder your computations, as long as you apply it consistently. Table 4-5 shows the addition of the column marked "Environmental Adjustment".

Table 4-5 Computing the Environmental Adjustment

Organizational Tasks	Criticality	Vulnerability	Threat	Risk	Environment Adjustment	Adj Risk(1)
Product Design	8	6	7	330	0.9	297
Product Development	8	5	6	250	0.2	50
Manufacturing	8	5	7	280	0.4	112
Measurement & Testing	8	4	7	216	0.5	108
Internal Movement	5	5	6	159	0.3	48
Warehousing	7	6	6	236	0.7	165
Marketing	4	7	5	151	0.9	135
Accounting	5	6	6	165	0.8	132
Planning	8	5	6	225	0.3	68
Shipping	5	4	6	128	0.3	38
Receiving	4	7	6	165	0.5	82
Misc. Clerical	4	5	6	110	0.6	66
Order Processing	4	5	6	120	0.7	84
Customer Sales & Service	7	6	6	242	0.5	121
Document Retrieval	8	6	6	282	1.1	310
Command & Control	4	6	6	138	0.3	41
Data Analysis	5	6	6	184	0.3	55
General Management	5	6	6	184	0.3	55

Graphing unadjusted and adjusted risk

Now, you can quantify the impact of the environmental factors and get a more accurate assessment of the risk involved, displaying the impact graphically as shown in figure 4-1.

Note the bars for "Shipping", where environmental factors (e.g., adverse flying conditions) make the risk greater.

Figure 4-1 Unadjusted and adjusted risk

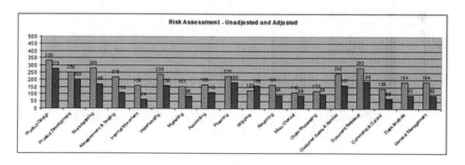

Advanced risk assessment #2: Identifying and assessing potential courses of action – now comes the fun

Identifying threats, criticalities, and vulnerabilities in accordance with a standard set of numerical values to provide a "snapshot" of operations is normally the extent of the basic risk assessment process. However, risk *assessment* becomes risk *management* when the CEO goes beyond what he has just completed, to identify and evaluate potential courses of action (COAs) before any time or funding is expended (or wasted). [10]

Implementing a new course of action to an existing mission, operation, or project does not change the **threat** to the mission. Neither does it change the **criticality** of the mission. It does (or should), however, change the **vulnerability** of the mission in the organization.

We now employ the following formula to show the impact of the course of action on the risk:

$$Risk = Threat \ x \ Criticality \ x \ \underline{Revised} \ Vulnerability \\ x \ Environmental \ Adjustment$$

Identifying potential COAs and modeling them in the risk assessment can be expected to show:

- Significant reductions of risk in one or more capability areas if implemented (good)
- Small or insignificant risk reductions if implemented (neither good nor bad)
- A potential increase in risk in another part of the mission if implemented (bad).

Table 3-6 takes the basic risk computation we did earlier but goes on to reflect the impact of the external environment (for better or worse) and the impact of the revised vulnerability. You now have a real snapshot of the present and your best possible prediction (albeit subjective) of the future – if you implement a particular course of action (or series of courses of action). [11]

---

[10] Get set to blow the socks off the Board of Directors.
[11] Again, the shaded columns are computed automatically.

Table 4-6 Computing risk after COA implementation

Organizational Tasks	Criticality	Vulnerability	Threat	Risk	Environment Adjustment	Adj Risk(1)	Revised Vulnerability	Adj Risk(2) (COA)
Product Design	8	6	7	330	0.9	297	5	248
Product Development	8	5	6	250	0.2	50	4	40
Manufacturing	8	5	7	280	0.4	112	3	67
Measurement & Testing	8	4	7	216	0.5	108	2	54
Internal Movement	5	5	6	159	0.3	48	2	19
Warehousing	7	6	6	236	0.7	165	4	110
Marketing	4	7	5	151	0.9	135	4	77
Accounting	5	6	6	165	0.8	132	4	88
Planning	8	5	6	225	0.3	68	4	54
Shipping	5	4	6	128	0.3	38	5	48
Receiving	4	7	6	165	0.5	82	4	47
Misc. Clerical	4	5	6	110	0.6	66	4	53
Order Processing	4	5	6	120	0.7	84	4	67
Customer Sales & Service	7	6	6	242	0.5	121	4	81
Document Retrieval	8	6	6	282	1.1	310	4	207
Command & Control	4	6	6	138	0.3	41	3	21
Data Analysis	5	6	6	184	0.3	55	3	28
General Management	5	6	6	184	0.3	55	3	28

Risk assessment at a glance – telling the story

If you work with spreadsheets, you already know how to create and revise graphs automatically. [12] Figure 3-2, the automatically developed graph shows:

- The unadjusted (basic) risk assessment
- The impact (for better or worse) of the external environment on the assessed risk
- The impact of a notional course of action, which is the result of revising the numerical value for *vulnerability*.

Figure 4-2 The Total Risk Management Picture

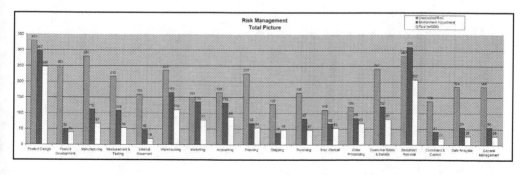

---

[12] Once constructed, the graph changes automatically when the values in the table change.

Again, our figures are notional in order to show the utility of the model and to suggest that all relevant factors need to be considered. They are not from any specific project.

It is not unusual to discover that simulating the implementation of potential courses of action (i.e., "gaming" them) predicts only small or insignificant changes. That's OK! In fact, modeling can show the CEO that certain courses of action may not be worth the time or expense. You need to know that before you waste time and money. It is also a good way to impress your bosses or the Board.

The Rest of the Story – Describing Urgency

Having done all the work, it remains to tell the rest of the story by defining "urgency". That is, which are the highest risks and, therefore, the most urgent to correct or mitigate. We will do that with a simple stoplight chart, developed as follows:

1. The highest number we developed in the risk assessment process was 330.
2. We want to create three categories of urgency: Critical, Necessary, and Routine, shown in red, yellow, and green respectively[13].
3. Accordingly, we divide 1- 330 in three equal parts (1-110, 111-220, and 221-330).

Table 4-7 describes the categories of urgency.

Table 4-7 Creating Categories of Urgency

Organizational Tasks	Urgency
221-330	Critical
111-220	Necessary
1-110	Routine

---

[13] I left in the labels in case the color differences were not obvious.

Table 4-8 is the final table and stoplight chart as shown below.

Table 4-8 Risk Urgency Chart

Organizational Tasks	Risk	Env. Adj	COA	Adj. Risk	After COA
Product Design	330	297	248	Critical	Critical
Product Development	250	50	40	Routine	Routine
Manufacturing	280	112	67	Necessary	Routine
Measurement & Testing	216	108	54	Routine	Routine
Internal Movement	159	48	19	Routine	Routine
Warehousing	236	165	110	Necessary	Routine
Marketing	151	135	77	Necessary	Routine
Accounting	165	132	88	Necessary	Routine
Planning	225	68	54	Routine	Routine
Shipping	128	38	48	Routine	Routine
Receiving	165	82	47	Routine	Routine
Misc. Clerical	110	66	53	Routine	Routine
Order Processing	120	84	67	Routine	Routine
Customer Sales & Service	242	121	81	Necessary	Routine
Document Retrieval	282	310	207	Critical	Necessary
Command & Control	138	41	21	Routine	Routine
Data Analysis	184	55	28	Routine	Routine
General Management	184	55	28	Routine	Routine

Note the following:

- We automatically apply the environmental adjustments to the "Urgency".
- The risk mitigations developed for "Product Design" are insufficient. Either greater mitigation will be needed or the effort and expense involved will be assigned to something else.
- Risk mitigation in the area of "Document Retrieval" can reduce the urgency of the risk from urgent to necessary.
- Mitigation is expected to change the urgency of five tasks from Necessary to Routine.

Many tasks are already within our definition of routine urgency (as shown in green). According to our criteria, further correction or mitigation can be achieved with only routine effort.

Potential Benefits of a Structured Risk Management Process

Here is a summary of the potential benefits of conducting structured risk assessments in your organization.

1. Risks are identified, as well as their effects and interactions.
2. Contingency plans/courses of action can be developed, including preemptive responses which mitigate or reduce the potential impacts.
3. Expected costs can reduced, and an appropriate balance between costs and risk exposure achieved, usually with a reduced risk exposure.
4. Feedback into the design phases and planning stages is developed as part of the evaluation of risk vs. expected cost balance.
5. Opportunities and responses are recognized and gamed in advance.
6. The integration of planning and cost control is improved.
7. Members of the project team develop an analytical understanding of the likely problems and responses in their own areas, and problems in other areas which will impact on them.
8. Specific problem areas are highlighted for further analysis.
9. Management is provided with a means of signaling trends without redefining objectives.
10. Knowledge and judgments are formalized and documented, making projects easier to manage throughout their life cycles.
11. External technical, environmental, and political influences are specifically measured in direct relation to internal issues, and appropriate strategies are developed reflecting both.
12. Probability distributions are can be developed for estimating costs and completion dates.

3. Security Risk Assessment

Security Risk Assessment, like any other focused risk assessment, requires the identification and assessment of the *threats, criticalities,* and *vulnerabilities* of the organization and its missions. The organization must establish and maintain a strategy for the ongoing identification, assessment, and mitigation of all its risks, including those related to organizational security. Mitigation means the identification and implementation of effective control measures or courses of action.

4. Security Risk Management

It is in the execution (or gaming) of the control measures that risk *assessment* becomes risk *management*. We identify notional threats, apply them to different sub-tasks, and assign numerical values in the following table[14].

Table 4-9 Listing and computing threats

SECURITY TASKS	Terrorist Attack	Utility Loss	Hacker/Cyber Attack	Industrial Espionage	Strike	Agent Spill	Natural Disaster	Falsified reporting	Total	Average
1. Security/Surveillance										
Detecting/identifying unauthorized movement - personnel	9	4	9	9	3	5	8	8	55	7
Detecting/identifying unauthorized movement - vehicles	9	4	9	9	3	5	8	8	55	7
Surveillance of restricted areas	4	4	9	9	3	5	8	8	50	6
Securing incident sites	9	9	9	5	3	5	8	8	56	7
Detection of unauthorized material	9	4	9	5	6	5	8	8	54	7
Surveillance of facility access points	9	4	6	5	6	5	8	8	51	6
Harbor surveillance	6	4	6	5	3	5	8	8	45	6
Automatic security systems	4	4	6	5	3	5	8	8	43	5

Table 3-10 describes risk assessment of those same security sub-tasks. The bars reflect successively taking mitigations into account according to the following steps:

1. *Risk = Threat x Criticality x Vulnerability*
2. *Adjusted Risk = Threat x Criticality x Vulnerability x Environmental Adjustment*
3. *Predicted Risk = Threat x Criticality x Revised Vulnerability x Environmental Adjustment.*

---

[14] This is the method that I have written about in my book and in professional journals. You may want to do it differently. It's only necessary to be <u>consistent</u> throughout the risk assessment process.

Table 4-10 Computing Security Risk Management

Capabilities	Criticality Assessment	Vulnerability Assessment	Threat Assessment	Unadjusted Risk	Environmental Adjustment	Adjusted Risk	Revised Vulnerability	Adj Risk(2) (COA)
1. Security/Surveillance								
Detecting/identifying unauthorized personnel	8	6	7	336	0.5	168	3	84
Detecting/identifying unauthorized vehicles	2	5	7	70	0.4	28	3	17
Surveillance of restricted areas	3	8	6	144	0.2	29	5	18
Securing incident sites	3	6	7	126	0.3	38	4	25
Detection of unauthorized material	4	3	7	84	0.5	42	2	28
Surveillance of facility access points	4	2	6	48	0.2	10	2	10
Harbor surveillance	5	2	6	60	1.2	72	2	72
Automatic security systems	4	3	5	60	0.7	42	2	28

Expressed graphically in Figure 4-3:

Figure 4-3 The Security Risk Management picture

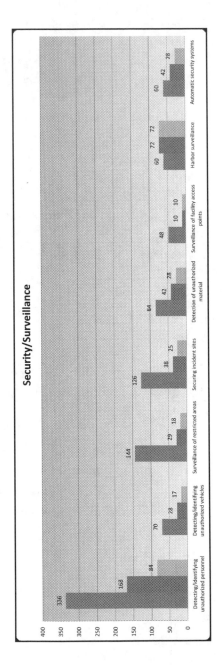

SUMMARY

A comprehensive security risk analysis should be performed in all departments of an organization regularly, including (and especially) the IT department. IT audits should evaluate the risk to the organization if computer systems fail, from either intentional or accidental forces; plus, how long the organization can function without computer services; and the ultimate costs (immediate and projected).

CHAPTER FIVE

Synergy vs. Innovation

This chapter is adapted from "Synergy – Innovation You Can Measure" an article I wrote some time ago for "Defense AT&L." It has application outside the Military as well as inside.

Innovation and creativity need to measurably prove themselves at the earliest stages of the planning process, before valuable time and funds are assigned to their fruition. They must be subjected to the rigors of structured analysis, the most exacting of which is determining what synergies are created or satisfied, and to what degree. Anything less impairs our ability to achieve and maintain maximum performance, safety, and effectiveness.

Webster defines "innovation" as something new or different introduced, and as the introduction of new things or methods. Stakeholders want "innovation" both for and from organizations. But, if you're a manager:

- What does innovation look like?
- How do you know when you've been innovative?
- How do you know if the innovation (once identified) will do any good, especially if you're talking about spending a large amount of time and funding to develop it?
- How much good will it do for the amount of time and funding invested?
- How do you know that a gain in one area won't result in an attendant loss in another?

Many pages later (and mercifully), Webster defines "*synergy*" as the combined or cooperative action of two or more stimuli for an enhanced effect. It means that the whole becomes *greater* than the sum of its parts, and that 1 + 1 can equal 2.5.

In business, synergy can mean that when separate departments within an organization cooperate and interact, they become more productive and efficient than if they had operated separately. For example, it is more efficient for each department in a small organization to deal with one finance department, rather than each requiring a finance department of its own.

We can work more effectively with synergy than with innovation because **synergy can be quantified**, whereas innovation (if not the result of pursuing synergy) often cannot. This chapter discusses synergy in general and representative synergies, how to look for synergies, and how to measure their effectiveness. It attempts to prove that the pursuit of synergy is of greater practical value than the pursuit of innovation.

What is required for the identification of synergies, above all, is a mindset. That is, a semi-automatic response from program managers that says one plus one must equal something *greater* than 2.0, or it's not worth the doing.

1. Evolving Synergy

> **Redundancy ➡Commonality ➡ Synergy**

In the development of synergies, the Program Manager[15] must look for three progressively supporting behaviors:

- *Redundancy*: wherein several organizations perform *similar* activities to achieve the same objectives; leading to
- *Commonality*: wherein several organizations perform *the same* activities to achieve the same objectives; leading to
- *Synergy*: wherein one organization, by doing one activity for several similar organizations, achieves more than could be accomplished by all the similar organizations each doing the same activity.

---

[15] More properly, the Program Manager and his/her staff.

EUGENE A. RAZZETTI

Too often, acquisition processes stop at commonality, confusing it with both innovation and synergy. Acquisition has come too far and the need is too great to be content only with commonality. Commonality is a poor substitute for either synergy or innovation.

2. What we mean by Synergy and how we know when we've got it

For our purposes, synergy refers to the measurable behavior of whole systems not predicted by the behavior of their component parts taken separately. Synergy can play a vital role in planning and financing the conduct of modern business. Management deals with how (and to what degree) to integrate those capabilities and assets of diverse organizations and how combining capabilities can create something greater than their total.

Successful synergistic culture change builds upon the strengths of the organization's components. Organizations have the potential for high degrees of synergy. However, in terms of population, assets, and capabilities, their optimization remains elusive. Organizations must develop or combine their material and non-material assets synergistically, in order to achieve and maintain optimal performance of systems and maximum safety and effectiveness for warfighters.

3. Synergy Identification

There have been many long and scholarly books on the subject of strategic *planning*, but comparatively little meaningful guidance on the *creation* of strategy. Accordingly, making synergy identification both an objective and an agenda item in strategic planning may provide needed structure to the strategy creation process. Identification of synergies should be as early as possible in the strategic planning process, as shown in figure 5-1.

Figure 5-1 The role of synergy identification in planning and acquisition

Regrettably, program managers may have little or no control of initial threat and assessment or during strategic planning. Thus, synergy identification may not occur prior to commencement of the acquisition process. It is imperative to identify the synergies and their associated metrics at the earliest point in an acquisition process, in order to shape and control technology development.

The synergies (and their associated metrics) should be locked in during Concept Decision and revisited throughout the acquisition process. The Program Manager needs a robust, pre-approved set of synergies and metrics in order to shape concept design, and to direct (and limit) technology development. Synergies also provide continuing guidance and feedback during the acquisition and sustainment stages, providing decision (i.e., go/no go) criteria for program initiatives.

4. Synergy + Metrics = Objectives

Implementing synergies begins with aligning them and their associated metrics with the gaps or shortcomings to be addressed in the acquisition, and developing the objectives of the acquisition. Threat and risk assessments, if properly conducted, should provide the required specificity for identifying the requirements and the synergies, and for planning the acquisition.

Let's assume that we need a watercraft to perform two related missions. One mission requires a cruising speed of only 15 knots. The other mission requires a maximum sustained transit speed of 25 knots.[16] Proper analysis

---

[16] These two speed figures are for demonstration and do not reflect any actual programs or analyses.

by operators and engineers confirms that a single watercraft capable of 25 knots can perform both missions. The development of a watercraft capable of 25-knots is now a defensible objective (or top-level requirement) for program management personnel charged with design and construction of the watercraft.

Table 5-1 Synergy Spreadsheet (Simplified)

Number	Capability Affected	Identified By	Gap	COA	Metric	Synergies
As assigned	Search and Rescue	Department Head	Existing craft too slow	Develop a faster watercraft	Speed (kts) Cruising Range (nm) Sensor range (nm)	Force Multiplication

The ability of the watercraft to achieve the desired synergy is therefore (along with a great many other things, of course) a function of its ability to achieve and maintain a minimum top speed of 25 knots.

SUMMARY

The intent of this chapter is to stress the importance of the synergy "mindset" in management in general and security in particular. It is not to trivialize the importance of innovation or (for that matter) creativity. Both of these less tangible virtues need to measurably prove themselves at the earliest stages of the acquisition process, before valuable time and funds are assigned. Innovation must be subjected to the rigors of structured analysis, the most exacting of which is determining what synergies are created or satisfied, and to what degree.

Organizations must identify and pursue potential synergies as early as possible for systems yet to be developed. They also must develop or combine existing material and non-material assets synergistically. Anything less impairs their ability to achieve and maintain maximum performance from systems and ensure maximum effectiveness. If the innovations are worth the doing, they will survive the scrutiny of the synergy identification process. And be welcomed.

CHAPTER SIX

System Integration - Enabling Capability Through Connectivity

> *When you audit a system integration plan, you audit an entire program – cradle to grave*

System Integration is both a component and a byproduct of successful program management and should be included in any audit strategy. It isn't rocket science, but it is challenging, and, according to certain studies, up to 70 percent of system integration projects fail or fall short in some part. When program managers stay focused on system integration throughout the program, and not as an end-of-pipe activity, successful integration of subsystems into a finalized system is almost certain. A "System Integration Plan" will write, revise and continually improve itself. When you audit a system integration plan, you audit an entire program.

System Integration and Program Management

System Integration is the process of bringing together the component sub-systems into one system. It is an aggregation of subsystems cooperating so that the resultant system is able to deliver an overarching functionality or capability by ensuring that the subsystems function together as *one* system.

In information technology, this is the process of linking together different computing systems and software applications physically or functionally, to act as a coordinated whole. An integrated system streamlines processes, reduces costs, and increases efficiency.

System Integration connects multiple separate components — often from different sources — to work as one. Some subsystems are old, some are new. Program managers usually find that putting the subsystems together as early as possible in the program's development improves mission effectiveness and helps to ensure seamless *connectivity*, enabling commanders at the front and at the rear to better execute and assess strategic and tactical accomplishment.

Connectivity refers to a program's or device's ability to link with other programs or devices. For example, a program that can import data from a wide variety of sources and can export data in many different formats is said to have "good connectivity," especially when connecting to or communicating with another computer or computer system. The finest subsystems are useless (or at least fall short) if they cannot effectively connect with each other and form the system. Connectivity in decision making means harnessing information from many information generators (or sensors) into one total picture — often called the *Commander's Dashboard*.

System integration employs all the principles and practices of successful program management; there is virtually nothing that should be considered new, unique or *over and above*. Table 6-1 summarizes and compares the requirements of system integration with those of successful program management. The requirements are identical.

Table 6-1. Simultaneously auditing Systems Integration and Program Management

Requirement	Program Management	System Integration
Mission planning; concept development	✓	✓
Design/development (including hardware/software)	✓	✓
Modeling/Simulation	✓	✓
Research & development	✓	✓
Risk management plan	✓	✓
Gap analysis	✓	✓
Core team developed; responsibility/accountability assigned (including decision makers)	✓	✓
Warfighter involvement	✓	✓
Performance-oriented; metrics developed/consistent/actionable	✓	✓
Test plans developed; tech yield identified	✓	✓
Contract in place; executable	✓	✓
Connectivity/feedback	✓	✓
Configuration/change management process defined/in place	✓	✓
Internal/external security procedures in place	✓	✓
Life cycle management plan	✓	✓

Please note especially the inclusion of "warfighter involvement," "technological yield," and "connectivity." These requirements, often neglected in a program's early stages, are essential not only for managing the program but for ensuring that subsystems and components successfully address the mission and *integrate* into a viable end product ("e.g., a weapons system, with all hardware, software, training simulators, and supply support).

Research and Development—Another Way to Look at It

Past usage of the familiar and perhaps archaic term "Research and Development" or "R&D" has often suggested its detachment, and/or inclusion as an *end product* at the *beginning* of the design. "Acceptance testing" (an equally archaic term) often is thought to be at end of the development pipeline. Not integrating R&D and Acceptance Testing into the entire program invites disaster.

The alternative approach shown in Figure 6-1 depicts potential gain from a robust and ongoing integration/connectivity strategy in the R&D processes, where subsystems are measured continuously against system requirements. Acceptance testing is constant and actionable feedback is immediate. *Quality* testing throughout development replaces *quantity* testing at the end; and proactive configuration management replaces recalls and retrofits.

Figure 6-1. Research and Development Connectivity

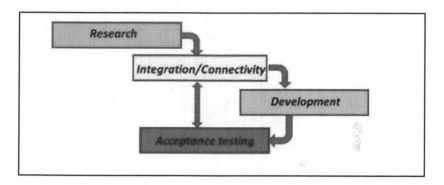

Subsystems are validated and tested. Test engineers, detecting any problems, can initiate timely corrective action. The subsystem again undergoes operational (acceptance) testing, to ensure that the subsystems come as close as possible to errorless performance.

Modeling and Simulation

In writing on the importance of modeling and simulation in wargames and/or tabletop exercises and as replacements for case studies, I need to stress two points:

1. Modeling and simulation should take place throughout the program.
2. Warfighters/operators should participate throughout the program.

Manufacturing and developmental process outcomes can be gamed— especially when dealing with the inevitable potential for reconfiguration and/or a change in operational requirements. Simulations can optimize projected human interactions, information collection, artificial intelligence, and data analyses. Modeling and simulation across all systems integration processes provide the timely feedback and alternative approaches for informed decision making. The greater the integration, the greater and more dynamic are the ability and effectiveness of the decisions.

With regard to warfighter/operator involvement, we need only remember that Department of Defense (DoD) programs, especially those involving our nation's offensive and defensive weapons systems, leave the most compelling risks to in-theater operators, and not program managers. Warfighter/operators need to be involved in the system integration.

Personnel

System integration requires dedicated, focused, professionals with exceptional expertise. Excellent technology is not enough if the required integration expertise is not there to implement it. Organizations may struggle to find and retain employees with the required skill sets for system integration. Contractors may advertise having expertise even if it does not yet exist, hoping to pick it up on the fly. An external or "third-party" specialist/consultant may bring needed integration expertise to the table more expeditiously.

Technological "Yield" —Potential into Performance

Technological "yield" refers to how measurably successful the essential technologies are integrated into the overall product architecture, application and user environment. The yield, as described in performance metrics such as miles per hour, target acquisition range, or mean time between failures, is a measure of how close *actual* performance comes to *theoretical* performance. A high yield suggests a successful integration of the technology. That said, technological yield findings are not always immediate, accurate or predictive. Subsequent testing and re-testing may produce lower values, suggesting that the technology may not yet be mature and, therefore not ready for production and/or implementation.

System Integration Process

There is no such thing as a *standard* system integration. Every system uses different subsystems to achieve different goals. The System Integrator (or team) must understand all the current and predicted program requirements. Translating program requirements into needs, and continuously improving communication between program management and the system integration team, connect the visions of the designers with the program managers' realities.

Figure 6-2 describes how the system integration process fits in the big picture of program management. Again, nothing in the process is beyond the requirements of effective program management.

Figure 6-2. The System integration Process

*All applicable general and specialty engineering disciplines (including safety and environmental)

** Command, Control, Communications, Computers/Intelligence, Surveillance, and Reconnaissance

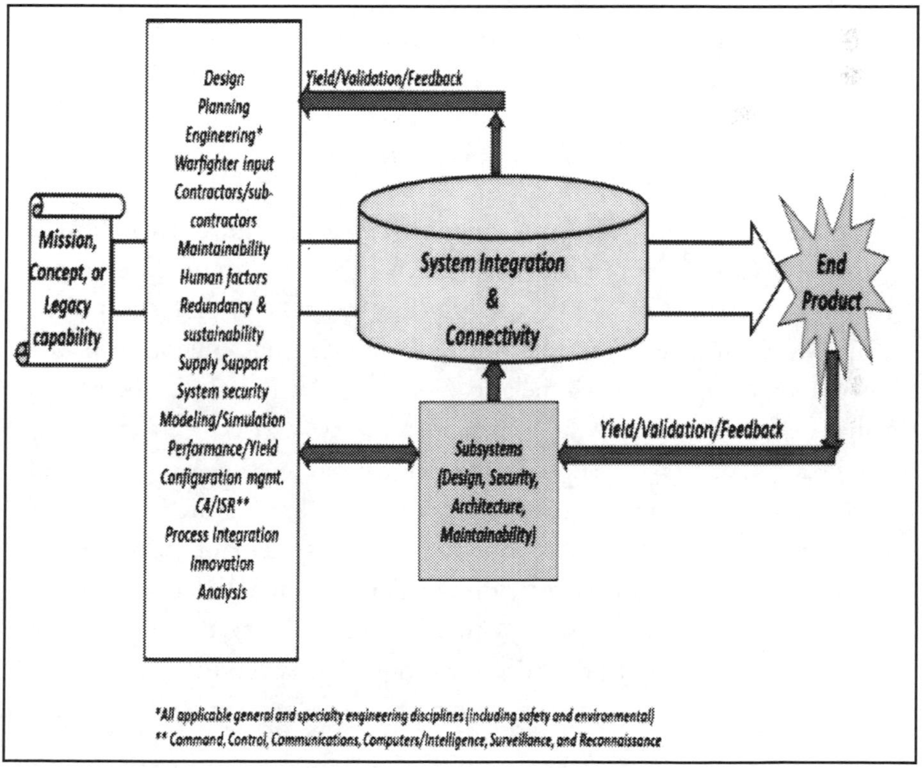

The task of integrating legacy or already-existing subsystems into new systems or capabilities can require much research and effort. Only in recent years have systems been deployed that can interconnect innovative and legacy subsystems. However, many systems and subsystems were "stovepipe" designs with no thought about future connectivity. Depending on their number and size, connecting several independent systems and subsystems into one while ensuring uninterrupted connectivity will take time and meticulousness. Successful system integration in the private sector helps forward-thinking companies to grow and prosper by automating many business processes and providing accurate decision-making data throughout.

The longest and the most challenging phase of the program can be where the actual integration is performed. Based on a logical architecture design, a physical equivalent is developed. If all previous steps have been followed with a close attention to detail, a system integrator should perform system integration successfully and easily, without losing valuable time, funding or data.

Design, Architecture and Maintainability

System integrators/teams must design the architecture to create strong foundations and to minimize risk as much as possible, in order to ensure that multiple subsystems and components function as one. Only then will the system meet (or exceed) mission requirements. Blueprints of the integration components will help to visualize the process(es). The goal is enhanced efficiency and seamless data connectivity.

Program managers should consider having subsystems integrated by professional integrators, rather than buying "off-the-shelf" solutions implemented by unqualified contractors. If a system or subsystem is difficult to operate or deficient, the integrator should initiate corrective action immediately. If and when a mission evolves, the system must evolve with it. Also, there may be no need to acquire a new product, as it can be more beneficial to upgrade the system you already know and find easy to use.

Secure System Integration in today's world

Virtually every complex system in use in America today has or could have a government or Military function. Accordingly, it must be securely maintained, throughout its life cycle.

Department of Defense (DoD) programs (now and forever) will depend on the most accurate and actionable information, securely collected, stored and displayed. DoD security systems must protect data, information, and the knowledge acquired therefrom from theft, sabotage, accidents, misuse, and ignorance. The greater that amount of data—the greater the security challenge. The threat of cyber-attack will be with us always, and DoD programs must function in a cyber-secure environment—from preliminary design through the entire life cycle. Lives may depend on it.

How is information *networked*? The Internet may seem an obvious answer, but it is increasingly vulnerable to denial of service, hacking and physical destruction of the key "hubs" A dedicated military communication system is the default solution, although bandwidth allocation and management create additional challenges for program managers.

Organizational "Inertia" and Lack of Accountability

System integration always involves multiple players as well as multiple subsystems. Accountability for the success (or failure) of the integration becomes blurred very easily when integrating many different subsystems. There can be multiple stakeholders (e.g., vendors, users, system owners, etc.), none of them ultimately responsible for the entire system integration. Each may only handle or carry at most about one piece of the integration and be unlikely to appreciate the big picture or have a sense of urgency for it. When something goes wrong, the situation turns almost immediately to finger pointing and blaming other parties instead of someone "owning" the integration. When a single party manages the system integration project, he or she is (often contractually) responsible and accountable for integration success, and there is no longer any ambiguity. Accountability replaces ambiguity.

Some decision makers elect to acquire new or off-the-shelf packages instead of integrating already existing subsystems. Contractors often procure only the components that they actually need at the moment or to solve an immediate problem. This way may be faster and cheaper in the beginning, and thus seem more profitable and efficient. But the practice can very quickly become counterproductive, as the new additions become obsolete or create interoperability problems down the road. As the program evolves, it may start using more and more independent, free-standing, tools, possibly resulting in productivity decline and inaccurate/inconsistent data analyses. The longer the project takes, the more significant this issue becomes. Records become confusing and incapable of audit. Funds are used faster or are prematurely exhausted. Problem correction is funded from other finding lines or kicked to the next fiscal year. Keeping the integration projects as short as possible can improve program success. Furthermore, an agile working methodology that can address changing requirements along the way and also after the project is essential for systems integration success.

The "good" news, remember, is that system integration *is* program management; and the program manager is in charge. He or she controls the funds, owns the integration and establishes subordinate responsibility and accountability accordingly. The challenge to program managers is the time-consuming and complicated nature of integrating various subsystems.

Problem-Solving and Continual Improvement

We cannot discuss day-in, day-out program management and system integration without discussing two indispensable "mindsets." A *problem-solving* mindset accepts the fact that problems are inevitable but that any problem can be corrected—and, if not corrected entirely, in some way mitigated. *"Don't fix the blame, fix the problem"* should be the reaction; appreciating that a problem, once identified, is half solved. International Quality Management Standards such as ISO 9001:2015 instruct that selected corrective actions should be realistic and measurable, and that follow-up must ensure that the corrective actions produced the desired results.

Closely related is the *continual improvement* mindset that reminds program managers that any system or process, however efficient, can always be made better. The program managers must always be on the lookout for opportunities to improve a system, process or situation.

Outside auditors measure the continual improvement mindset in an organization by assessing:

- Adherence to policies and objectives
- Analysis of data and effectiveness or recurring reports
- Effectiveness of following up previous corrective and preventive actions
- Structured program reviews, with actionable findings, conclusions and recommendations.

SUMMARY

There are essentially no more stand-alone operations or weapons. DoD programs, especially those involving our nation's offensive and defensive weapons systems, leave the most compelling risks and decisions to in-theater operators, not to stateside program managers or contractors. Connectivity in decision making means harnessing information from many information generators (or sensors) into one total picture.

Successful system integration and the need to streamline processes for more effective program management and warfighting is more important now than ever, due to the increasing advances in warfighting technology among major powers and the pernicious adventurism of a few thug nations.

Comprehensive program management creates, in its execution, successful system integration. Program managers need to stay focused on system integration throughout a program, and not as an end-of-pipe activity. Only then will integration of subsystems into a finalized system be possible.

CHAPTER SEVEN

Some Additional Thoughts about Internal Auditing Before We Discuss Security

Management consultants (like me) routinely help to set up or reorganize companies in order to help them to reach their full potential. With a little more effort, some of us give them the *ongoing* capability to effectively audit themselves, and to improve themselves on a continuing basis.

Points to Remember

✓ An "audit" is a systematic, independent, and documented process for obtaining audit evidence and evaluating it objectively to determine the extent to which audit criteria are fulfilled. "Internal audits" are audits conducted by on behalf of the organization itself for internal purposes, and can form the basis of the organizations self-declaration of conformity (compliance).

✓ Developing an internal (self) auditing capability within an organization is vital to the continued success of that organization.

✓ A well-planned, effective, internal auditing program should consider the relative importance of the processes and areas to be audited.

✓ The success of an organization is the sum of the effectiveness of management authority, responsibility, and accountability. They are, in turn, the sum of the manner in which management deals with the findings of the internal audits.

Management consultants, who can audit processes and train organizations to audit themselves, can be heroes to their clients, as well as permanent "value-adds". Audits provide practical, impartial, feedback, and can save large amounts of time and money. Structured, proven, international management standards such as ISOs 9000, 14000, 27000, and 28000 heighten the value of effective *internal* auditing of organizational processes, toward a goal of continuous improvement. An organization must be able to swiftly identify and correct its own shortcomings, without relying on outsiders. Developing an internal auditing capability within a client organization can be as important to the continued success of that organization as the consulting engagement itself. More than ever, organizations must satisfy themselves and their stakeholders that they are as secure as possible from threat and attack. Moreover, they must realize that security can be more important than profitability.

Years ago, one of my many and often-frustrated mentors[17] had a sign in his office that read: "***Expect What You Inspect***". That meant, as he "patiently" explained: "If you check on something routinely, before long you will be happy with what you see. If you hardly ever check it, you'll likely be unhappy when finally *forced* not only to look at it, but also to fix it, and if you inspect frequently, the area or function eventually operates well and continues to improve". Outside auditors audit against known standards, internal auditors should do the same.

Looking critically at internal operations and processes and comparing them with approved standards is the basis of internal auditing. An organization can develop its own internal auditing capability, or (you guessed it) can hire a management consultant. Either way, an effective program of internal auditing provides a comprehensive, self-sustaining, evaluation and improvement capability for an organization. Its structure and administration can be inexpensive, but its contribution can be priceless to the client, as well as satisfying (and lucrative) to the consultant.

Organizations don't always do all the work required to establish effective internal auditing programs or adequately qualify internal auditors. As a result, audits tend to be perfunctory, biased, or sporadic. More important, critical audit findings may not be declared (and corrective actions not instituted). Instead of executing a meaningful measure of

---

[17] Often frustrated by me, I'm afraid.

organizational effectiveness, unqualified and unmotivated auditors only waste time, annoy busy people, and turn everyone off to the potential benefits of internal auditing.

Auditing to "Approved Standards"

"Quality," in its most simplistic definition, is conformance with standards. Approved process standards are vital to the continuous improvement and competitiveness of an organization. They form the criteria with which meaningful self-assessment can be made.

The ever-changing global marketplace has placed great emphasis on the importance of quality in all goods and services.[18]

Internal Auditing

The best way to describe internal auditing is with two definitions from the ISO 9000 Standard.[19]

- An "audit" is a systematic, independent, and documented process for obtaining audit evidence and evaluating it objectively to determine the extent to which audit criteria are fulfilled.
- "Internal audits" are audits conducted by on behalf of the organization (client) itself for internal purposes, and can form the basis of the organizations self-declaration of conformity (compliance).

Properly planned and well-implemented internal audits provide management with an ongoing, credible, and structured measure of how well the organization is achieving its goals and objectives.

---

[18] The Malcolm Baldridge National Quality Improvement Act of 1987 (Pub L 100-107), signed by President Reagan, established the Malcolm Baldridge National Quality Award, named in honor of the Secretary of Commerce. This award is presented to organizations who have achieved excellence in their endeavors, as assessed by established evaluation standards and criteria.

[19] American Society for Quality, ANSI/ISO/ASQ Q 9001 – 2008 Standard, Quality Press, Milwaukee, WI, 2008

> *Remember: Management can identify its own problems, or it can hear about them from customers; and if those problems involve security, Management might not get a second chance.*

What does an Internal Audit look like?

Here are some characteristics of an effective internal audit program. I'll start with the obligatory acronym - that way we'll get it over with:

"SMART": Scheduled – Measurable – Accurate – Repeatable – Timely.

There, that wasn't so bad.

The first step is to define and *schedule* every "audit-able" process for an audit at least once per year. "Surprise" audits are marginally effective, upset auditees, and reinforce a "pass-fail" mindset. Processes compared against approved standards (pounds of waste produced, finished products per hour, etc.) are **measurable.** Checklists are important for audit structure and repeatability[20]. Audit findings are therefore **accurate.** Findings generated during the audit must be **repeatable**. That is, a different auditor, auditing to the same standard, should come up with the same findings.

Last, the audit should be **timely.** Discovering a problem that occurred six months ago, or has been occurring regularly for the last six months is not as good as finding it early. As a manager, you already knew that. Sorry!

Internal auditors should be independent of the processes being audited, and should never audit their own work. Some of an auditor's (or a consultant's) most challenging moments can be trying to assure middle managers that their jobs will not be jeopardized or forfeit as a result of audit findings. To do this with genuine credibility requires real, continuing, and committed support from Top Management. A commitment to continual improvement cannot exist in an atmosphere of retribution or retaliation. It just drives the troops deeper into the foxholes.

---

[20] Please see the checklists in the Appendix.

The internal auditing program (especially as it involves organizational security) must be organization-specific, to ensure compatibility with the other management systems in the organization. A "cookie-cutter" or plagiarized system will achieve only limited success at best. For this reason, international quality standards, like the ISO Standards, provide only "guidelines," and leave the client organization to fill in specifics. Additionally, a well-planned, effective, internal auditing program should consider the relative importance of the processes and areas to be audited. That is, *do first things first.*

The first thing an experienced auditor does is review of results of the last audit. Specifically:

- When was the last audit;
- What were the findings;
- Were preventive or corrective actions developed and implemented, and
- Were the preventive or corrective actions effective?

This says a great deal about how seriously the organization takes its auditing function.

What benefits can Internal Auditing bring to the organization?

Summarized below are key areas of management that can be improved by an effective internal auditing program. Look through these, and as you do, please think of how they apply to your organization.

Auditing Continuous Improvement

The ISO International Management Standards require Management to use the findings from internal audits to develop and implement improvements to the existing processes on a continuous basis. The premise is that every process can be improved, and that no process is ever "finished" or "completed." Auditing of processes (depending on the capability of the auditor) will nearly always result in the identification of deficiencies and recommendations for improvement. Management can constantly improve its operations, or it can hear about shortcomings from the customers.

Auditing Process Measurement and Confirmation

Management can use findings from internal audits for measurement, analyses, and improvement of existing processes; and to ensure conformance to established standards, contract requirements, regulatory requirements, as well as achievement of top management goals and objectives (e.g., reducing hazardous waste). Modern quality management system auditing goes beyond the earlier quality control or quality assurance expectations, which focused on adherence to customer contract specifications through individual disciplines (e.g., purchasing, inventory control, statistical techniques, etc.) rather than overall processes. Well-constructed internal audits can measure conformance to customer requirements, but they can also check customer communication and feedback (see below). [21]

Auditing Strategic Planning

Executing strategic plans requires taking broad plans and policies and translating them into discrete, measurable, components. Internal auditing of the Strategic Plan evaluates the organization's progress in meeting those components. Policies with vague goals and objectives, or unquantifiable performance measurements, become "paper" policies, and lead to personnel discouragement, customer dissatisfaction, and organizational failure.

Auditing the Raising of Problems to Management Attention

Modern internal auditing assesses the day-to-day effectiveness of organizations in measurable terms (delivery dates, rejects, recycled material, unit costs, etc.). It spotlights specific practices or procedures which may require increased management attention. Human resources management audits evaluate personnel structure in terms of qualifications, training, numbers, and functions versus needs. Internal auditing helps to evaluate

---

[21] What I also recommend that clients do (besides hire me) is to contact the American Society for Quality (ASQ). ASQ provides via website (http://standardsgroup. asq.org) a host of books, periodicals, and schedules of internal auditor training courses for companies interested in developing or improving their programs and initiatives. I am a member and have always been very pleased with the technical support I have received.

facilities (e.g., floor space, computer systems/LAN, heavy machinery, etc.) in terms of adequacy and conformance. All this is meaningless, however, if audit findings do not receive management attention and actionable corrections are not generated. There must be (as the ISO Standards require) structured management review, corrective action, feedback, follow-up, and accountability processes.

SUMMARY

The success of an organization is the sum of the effectiveness of management authority, responsibility, and accountability. They are, in turn, the sum of the manner in which management deals with the findings of the internal audits.

A management consultant whose strengths lie not only in the application of structured skills, but in objectivity, can effectively audit an organization, and also develop a team of auditors to conduct scheduled internal audits routinely, after he/she has gone on to other challenges. I believe that providing an organization with an effective self-auditing program is my best contribution.

SECTION TWO

Organizational Security Management

CHAPTER EIGHT

Auditing Organizational Security at Your Command

Managing organizational security is no different from managing any other of the Command's missions. Establish your policies, goals, and risk parameters; implement, train, measure, and benchmark. And then: audit, audit, audit.

Today, more than ever, Organizational Security is an essential component of a robust, responsive, Military command, and commands that cannot execute their operations in a self-imposed and self-monitored secure environment may cease to be effective at best, or cease to exist at worst - just as certainly as civilian organizations that cannot maintain operational effectiveness, profitability, or product superiority, only faster.

Organizations must *harden* their operations to protect them from either incidental or deliberate attack. Internal (i.e., self) auditing is essential to the hardening process.

Cybersecurity, the concept most frequently promoted these days, refers to a body of technologies, processes, and practices designed to protect networks, computers, programs and data from attack, damage, or unauthorized access. Is cybersecurity important and necessary? Of course, it is! However, cybersecurity should not be thought of as independent or self-standing.

Cybersecurity is an indispensable element of *Organizational Security,* which is the subject of this article.

Figure 8-1 describes the many organizational security-related challenges that Military commands (including cybersecurity) confront in the transition from planning to executing their missions.

Figure 8- 1 The Big Picture: Organizational Security in mission execution

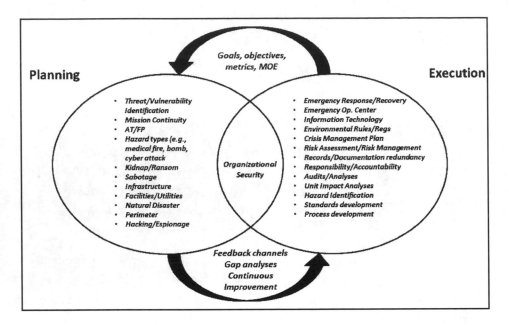

Several years ago, I worked as a Military Analyst on programs that included (like all modern Defense programs) *Information Warfare.* The lesson I continually re-learned during that time was that: ***Information is the only "weapon" that can be in more than one place at the same time.***

As Information Technology (IT) becomes increasingly integrated with *physical* infrastructure, there is increased risk for wide scale or high-consequence events that could cause harm or disrupt Military commands and their missions. In light of this link, strengthening organizational security and resilience is critical.

All U.S. Military commands depend on IT systems and computer networks for essential operations and mission fulfillment. IT systems face large and diverse cyber threats that range from unsophisticated hackers to technically competent intruders using state-of-the-art intrusion techniques. Many malicious attacks are designed to steal information and disrupt, deny access to, degrade, or destroy, critical information systems or to render infrastructure (e.g., power plants) out of commission.

Internal and external auditing of organizational security programs can ensure compliance with requirements, and can sustain an acceptable level of impregnability. More importantly, however, generating preventive and corrective actions as a result of those audits, and reassessing goals and objectives based on audit findings, perpetuates *continual improvement* and helps to establish and maintain a robust security posture into the future – forever raising the bar and leaving the status quo in the rearview mirror. I recommend that commanders looking to establish and maintain a structured information systems security management program review this international management standard: *ISO 27000: Information Systems Security Management.*

The paragraphs that follow will discuss how a robust program of internal auditing of a command's organizational security hardens and protects Military operations under a structured organizational security management system, and how anything less jeopardizes the existence of the command, the capability of its leadership, and the fulfillment of its missions.

Here are ten auditable areas in which commands can create and sustain credible, effective, and secure management systems and strategies – for headquarters commands, subordinates in the field, and suppliers.

1. Policy Development

Commanders must develop, as applicable to the mission, written security policies that are:

- Consistent with the other policies of the organization and those of higher authority
- Specific to security objectives, targets, and programs to be produced
- Consistent with the organization's overall security threat and risk management strategy and the nature and scale of its operations
- Clear in their statement of overall/broad security management objectives

- Documented, implemented, and monitored
- Communicated to all levels and to third parties including contractors and visitors with the intent that these persons are made aware of their individual security-related obligations.

2. Program Management

Effectively managing any program means continually monitoring the effectiveness of projects, procurements, and suppliers, establishing metrics, and identifying potential problems early. Commands must assess all the functions they perform and expend their limited resources according to the amount of vulnerability reduced for the amount of expense, as shown in figure 8-2.

Figure 8-2 A Cost vs. Effectiveness matrix (example)

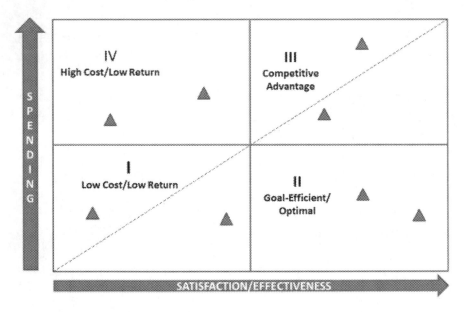

As the arrows suggest, you want to minimize funds committed to ineffective programs. The goal of the program management (with programs pictured as small pyramids) is to move programs into quadrants II and III. Programs in Quadrant I may appear acceptable, but can breed complacency, and there is no room for complacency in organizational security; not any more. Programs or projects that fall into Quadrant IV are unacceptable and require forthright (and likely unwelcomed) corrective action. Simultaneously, commanders must establish program management roles, responsibilities, and authorities, consistent with the achievement of the security management policies, objectives, and targets; and must communicate them.

Commanders need to commit, measurably and consistently, to development of a Security Management System (SMS) and to continually improving its effectiveness. Specifically:

- Communicating to the organization the importance of meeting its security management requirements in order to comply with its established policies
- Ensuring any security programs generated from other parts of the organization complement the security management system
- Communicating to the organization the importance of meeting its security management requirements in order to comply with its policy
- Establishing meaningful security metrics and measures of effectiveness
- Ensuring security-related threats, criticalities, and vulnerabilities are evaluated and included in organizational risk assessments as appropriate
- Ensuring the viability of the security management objectives, targets, and programs.

3. Security Risk Management

Security Risk Management, like any other focused risk management strategy, requires commanders to identify and assess "risk" in terms of *threats, criticalities*, and *vulnerabilities* to the commands and their missions. Commanders must establish and maintain strategies for the ongoing identification, assessment, and mitigation of all risks, especially those related to Organizational Security. *Mitigation* means to identify and implement effective control measures or courses of action. It is in the execution of the control measures that risk *assessment* becomes risk *management.* An effective Security Risk Assessment strategy should include identifying (as appropriate):

- Physical failure threats and risks, such as functional failure, incidental damage, malicious damage, or terrorist or criminal action
- Operational threats and risks, including the control of security, human factors, and other activities that affect the organization's performance, condition, or safety
- Factors outside of the organization's control such as failures in externally supplied (e.g., outsourced) equipment and services
- Security equipment, including replacement, maintenance, information and data management, and communications
- Any other threats to the continuity of operations.

4. Security Training &Qualification

Security-minded organizations appoint (and entrust) personnel to operate their security management systems. Like any other responsible positions in the Military, the people who design, operate, and manage the security equipment and processes must be suitably *qualified* in terms of education, training, certification, and/or experience. I put the word "qualified" in italics because *training* may not be enough. Commanders need qualification programs for all critical positions and watch stations, not just a training plan.

Further, all personnel must be fully aware and supportive of the importance of compliance with security management policies and procedures, and to the requirements of the Security Management System, as well as their roles in achieving compliance. This includes emergency preparedness and response, and the potential consequences to the organization's security by deviating from specified operating procedures.

5. Supply Chain Security

Every Military organization has a supply chain. Security requirements and attendant risks, which, whether upstream or downstream of its activities, can have a profound influence on operations, products, or services.

Identifying, evaluating, and mitigating threats posed from upstream or downstream supply chain activities is as essential as performing the same functions inside your own fence line, and commanders would do well to audit outside that fence line.

Commanders can effectively audit outside that fence line by (1) identifying all links/nodes of the supply chain and ensuring their conformance with stated security management policies, controls, and mitigation of threats posing unacceptable risks; (2) examining documented procedures governing situations where an absence of procedures could lead to failure to maintain operations; (3) the security requirements for contractor-furnished goods or services which impact on mission accomplishment; and (4) hardened and redundant lines of communication.

Where existing designs, installations, or operations are changed, documentation of changes should address attendant revisions to command structure, roles or responsibilities; security management policy, objectives, targets, or programs, processes or procedures, and the introduction of new security infrastructure, equipment, or technology.

Auditing of the supply chain also means auditing compliance with legal, statutory, and other regulatory security requirements, security management objectives, delivery of its security management programs, and the required level of security (convoys, containers, warehouses, etc.,) as appropriate. In my experience, there can be no control of the supply chain without a viable, robust, auditing function.

6. Communication & Documentation

Commands must have secure, hardened, and redundant procedures for disseminating all pertinent security management information. This applies to outsourced or host nation-provided operations as well as those taking place within the organization. This is especially important when dealing with sensitive or classified information.

Security management system documentation system includes but is not limited to:

- The Security Management System scope, policy, objectives, and targets

85

- Description of the main components of the security management system and their interaction, and reference to related documents
- Documents including records determined by the organization to be necessary to ensure the effective planning, operation and control of processes that relate to its significant security threats and risks.

7. Emergency Preparedness and Response

Emergency response may be thought of as conducting normal operations at faster-than-normal speeds, or it may mean something entirely different. The security-minded organization needs to establish, implement, and maintain appropriate plans and procedures (including backing up of records or files) for responses to security incidents and emergency situations, and to prevent and/or mitigate the likely consequences associated with them.

Auditing emergency plans and procedures should include all reviewing (and testing when necessary) information dealing with identified facilities or services that may be required during or after incidents or emergency situations, in order to maintain continuity of operations. The best emergency planning that I have ever seen was at U.S. Navy Bases along the Gulf Coast, where the threat (and likelihood) of hurricanes is perennial and immense.

Commanders and staffs should periodically "stress-test" the effectiveness of their emergency preparedness, response, and recovery plans and procedures, especially after the occurrence of incidents or emergency situations caused by security breaches and threats. They should test these procedures periodically (as applicable), to include scheduling drills, tabletops, and exercises, and developing lessons learned and corrective actions throughout the testing.

A supporting program of internal or outside security audits also confirm whether/not the organization is in compliance with relevant legislation and regulations, best practices, and in conformance with the policies and objectives of higher authority. As above, commands need to maintain records of results, findings, and required preventive and corrective actions.

Security-minded commanders and staffs can audit their security management plans, procedures, and capabilities. Security audits can include periodic reviews, testing, post-incident reports and lessons learned, performance evaluations, and exercises. Significant findings and observations, once properly evaluated or gamed, should be reflected in revisions or modifications.

8. Daily "quick-looks"

Here are some immediate feedback operational initiatives for forward-thinking and security-minded organizations trying to identify and mitigate (on a daily basis) their vulnerability to exploitation. Develop some checklists and "check" these out:

- Intrusion detection systems
- Fences, security lighting, natural barriers
- CCTV
- Computer backup systems; firewalls
- Roof and ventilation duct accessibility
- Construction materials and thickness requirements
- Installed firefighting systems
- Roads, alleys, and storm drains
- Parking areas
- Sewage treatment systems
- Locks, doors, and access control
- Identification management (i.e., employees, customers, vendors)
- Utilities (including uninterruptible power systems and emergency generators)
- Safes, desks, filing cabinets, controlled/exclusion areas
- HAZMAT generation, storage, and management
- Vehicle surveillance and security (including delivery and fuel trucks)
- Proximity of emergency services (e.g. fire, medical, police)
- Mail and package processing.

9. Preventive and Corrective Action

> **Audit ➡ Nonconformity ➡ P/C Action ➡ Corrected/Improved**

Auditors (by whatever name you give them) discover "nonconformities" during their audits. In doing so, they identify the need for either preventive or corrective action. Top management (hopefully) supports the audit findings and initiates preventive or corrective actions as appropriate along with feedback and follow-up to measure the success (or lack thereof) of the actions taken.

Audits of organizational security are no different than audits of any other management program. In fact, the need for prompt corrective action may be even more critical.

10. Continual Improvement

Continual Improvement is the basis and underpinning of the ISO International Standards. All processes must be thought of as ongoing and never at an "end state". Top management develops a continuous improvement *mindset* that says that we can always make something better. Continual improvement of organizational security in the Military requires commanders and staffs to review their security management systems at planned and frequent intervals, in order to ensure continuing suitability, adequacy, and effectiveness in an ever-changing environment. Security audits and reviews should include assessing opportunities for improvement and the attendant need for revising the security management system, including security policies and security objectives, plus threats and risks. Organizations already working with ISO 9000 and ISO 14000 can, with minimal effort, expand internal audits and management reviews to cover security and well as quality and environmental management.

SUMMARY

Information can be exploited in many ways, and auditing organizational security has tremendous potential for experienced commanders and staffs to harden their resources and missions. The opportunities for continual improvement from auditing are as limitless as cyberspace and as identifiable as office furniture.

Auditing of Organizational Security, either stand-alone or as part of other management audits should include:

- Cyber and physical plant security (including firewalls, motion sensors, lighting, sewage treatment systems, and perimeter fencing)
- Evaluations of compliance with legal and regulatory requirements, plus the requirements of higher authority
- Feedback and follow-up on preventive or corrective actions taken
- Day-to-day security performance of personnel assigned
- The extent to which stated objectives and targets have been met
- The Security Risk Assessment strategy
- The status of corrective and preventive actions, and/or follow-up actions from previous audits, management reviews, drills and exercises
- Changing threats, or circumstances and recommendations for improvement.

Organizational security must be part of every mission. Outputs from security audits should be the catalyst for any revisions to the Security Management System, together with cost/benefit analyses, schedules, risk revisions, and other justifications. Establish policies and procedures, identify threats, conduct risk assessments, implement processes, identify corrective actions, and establish a mindset of continual improvement. And audit.

An effective Security Risk Management strategy should include identifying (as appropriate):

- Physical failure threats and risks, such as functional failure, incidental damage, malicious damage, or terrorist or criminal action
- Operational threats and risks, including the control of security, human factors, and other activities that affect the organization's performance, condition, or safety
- Environmental or cultural aspects which may either enhance or impair security measures and equipment
- Factors outside of the organization's control such as failures in externally supplied (e.g., outsourced) equipment and services
- Stakeholder threats and risks, such as failure to meet regulatory requirements
- Security equipment, including replacement, maintenance, information and data management, and communications
- Any other threats to the continuity of operations.

Security Risk Management is the foundation of an organization's emergency management program. A properly conducted security risk assessment allows decisions to be made based on realistic scenario assumptions and provides justification for commitment of program resources.

CHAPTER NINE

Compliance, Continuity, and COVID

The Missions Continue – Regardless and Remotely

The COVID-19 Pandemic, also known internationally as the Coronavirus Pandemic, is an ongoing contagion of coronavirus disease 2019 (COVID-19), producing severe acute respiratory syndrome coronavirus 2 (SARS-CoV-2).

First identified in December 2019 in Wuhan, China, the outbreak was declared a Public Health Emergency of International Concern in January 2020 and a pandemic in March 2020. As of 6 November 2020, more than 48.8 million cases worldwide have been confirmed, with more than 1.23 million deaths attributed to COVID-19.

> *When the pandemic hit, fewer than 50%*
> *of US companies had a generic contingency*
> *plan and 10% had no plan at all.*

Whether an organization was well-prepared for a pandemic or it had no contingency plan in place, business disruption and disaster followed. Organizational leaders saw firsthand the fragility of business systems, operations and revenue streams witnessed the critical importance of risk awareness and preparedness, as well as the need for robust "Continuity Management" programs.

Today, DoD program managers and contractors face a dual challenge: (1) How do they ensure continuity in their programs before during, and after a major disruption such as a pandemic; and (2) How do they do it remotely. If it helps create a sense of urgency for program managers: think of COVID 19 as a *bio-weapon*.

This chapter discusses the importance of Continuity Management in both the public and the private sectors. Like the cyberattack threat, the Pandemic threat will forever be real; and DoD's response to it must be just as real.

> ### *Compliance without Continuity is worthless in a pandemic*

Compliance with the applicable DoD contract is (or should be) mandatory for contract award and execution. However, *compliance* alone doesn't guarantee the ability of an organization to successfully respond to and survive a major disruptive incident; especially one with the scope, duration, and severity of the COVID 19 Pandemic.

Compliance with contract specifications can (to some extent) provide the Program Manager with a good feeling about the contractor's past, and a good snapshot of the contractor today; but *not nearly enough about tomorrow.* That kind of good feeling comes only with a favorable assessment the contractor's ability to handle "tomorrow." In short: Compliance requires Continuity. Otherwise, there may not be a "tomorrow" for the program. No "new normal;" or any other kind for that matter.

Figure 9-1 describes the sequence from "normal" to "new normal," and the importance of continuity planning to recovery and restoration.

Figure 9-1 Continuity planning

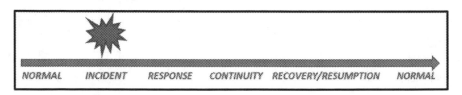

NORMAL   INCIDENT   RESPONSE   CONTINUITY   RECOVERY/RESUMPTION   NORMAL

I have written articles for DoD on the following distinct but related subjects over the last several years:

- Contingency Planning
- Adding COVID 19 to your Risk Management Model
- Collecting and analyzing "Lessons Learned"
- The importance of Second-Party Auditing
- Cybersecurity and System Integration in DoD
- Due diligence in DoD contracts and the courage to cancel a failed DoD program
- Lessons learned from Afghanistan
- Second party auditing of DoD contracts
- The value of Tabletop exercises.

When initially published, those articles were meant to help focus program managers on maximizing the effectiveness of both their programs' missions and their administration of them. Now, in light of the pandemic, my hope is that revisiting them will help to focus program managers on rebuilding programs damaged by the Pandemic; and to rebuild and operate them *remotely*, as the situations require.

Same challenge – different distance

The following terms will also help to assess continuity for future recoveries and structure the rebuilding required for recovery operations already in progress.

Continuity, for our purposes, means the ability to deliver previously agreed products and services even under extremely negative situations (e.g., during or after a natural disaster, terrorist act, or massive process failure). "Delivery" may be either to internal or external parties (e.g., between processes or to the end user).

Continuity management means a management process that covers the identification of situations that may have a high negative impact on DoD operations; and the implementation of capabilities and competencies, in order to properly respond to them and to protect the interest of DoD and other relevant interested parties.

Continual Improvement is the basis and underpinning of modern management. It must be thought of as an ongoing process and not an "end state".

It requires program managers and contractors to develop mindsets that we can always make something better.

Impact Analysis (IA) is a process that helps to identify the threats and effects that a disruption or serious situation can have on operations or activities. Impact analysis helps organizations to build resiliency and responsiveness into their operations.

A *Risk Management Plan* can be thought of as the end-user of the impact analysis. An organization's continuity management plan must have in place, a documented risk assessment process, in order to identify, analyze, evaluate, and treat risks that may lead to disruptive situations. Risk management (assessment and treatment criteria development) must consider the continuity plan's objectives and the organization's definition of acceptable risk.

Personnel awareness is an essential part of personnel competence. People who work under an organization's control must be made aware of the continuity policy and its contents, and what their personal performance means; plus, its objectives, and what the implications of nonconformities may be, and their roles during disruptive incidents. It's analogous to knowing the location and use of the closest fire extinguisher, fire alarm box, first aid kit, or eyewash station – only on a grander scale. And remotely.

Resources support continuity strategies. Organizations must define needed continuity resources, like people, information and data, buildings and facilities, equipment and consumable resources, transportation, suppliers, and partners.

Continuity Management Plan

A *Continuity Management Plan* is a set of procedures and instructions to guide an organization during and after a disruptive event; in order to speed up immediate response, recovery, and resumption of minimum operational conditions, and eventual restoration of normal operations. We must consider now the pandemic-driven requirement to assess and manage those management functions from a distance.

Table 9-1 compares normal DoD program management compliance functions with Continuity Management; then goes on to suggest that these functions may be monitored remotely. The requirements for compliance and continuity are essentially the same. It follows therefore that *continuity* in DoD programs must start at the very inception of the contract, and remain an integral part of it throughout. Normal and continuity management functions are identical; so it should not be a difficult shift to a "restoration" scenario if continuity was built into compliance at the beginning.

Table 9-1 Remotely monitoring compliance and continuity

Management Function	Compliance	Continuity	Monitor Remotely
Top management involvement	✓	✓	✓
Provision of resources	✓	✓	✓
Cost-benefit and risk analyses	✓	✓	✓
Preventive/corrective actions identified	✓	✓	✓
Internal audit	✓	✓	✓
Critical personnel/functions identified	✓	✓	✓
Recovery time objectives established	✓	✓	✓
Exercise (gaming potential disruptions	✓	✓	✓
Incident response structure	✓	✓	✓
Continual improvement	✓	✓	✓

The sections that follow expand on some of vital continuity management practices that already lend themselves to remote monitoring, and have done so for a long time.

Cost-Benefit Analysis

Cost-benefit analysis is a process with which businesses analyze decisions. The manager or analyst sums the benefits of a situation or action and then subtracts the costs associated with taking that action. Figure 9-2 describes the basic cost-benefit analysis process in action.

Figure 9 -2 Cost-benefit analysis

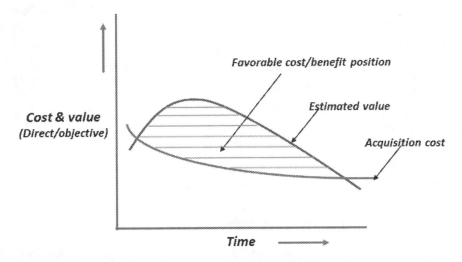

Thorough cost-benefit analyses reflect both objective (direct/easily quantified) and subjective (indirect/not easily quantified) costs and benefits. This can be done remotely, and revised whenever the situations change. Forward-thinking program managers are already doing cost-benefit analyses remotely.

Process approach

A Process Approach means managing a group of processes as a system, where the interrelations between processes are identified and the outputs of a previous process are treated as the inputs of the next one. The process approach helps to ensure that the results of each individual process will *add value* and contribute to achieving the final desired results. There should (theoretically) be no wasted or unnecessary operations. Process approaches also identify opportunities for potential synergy, innovation, risk identification, and resource reallocation. Even the most complicated processes may be analyzed and monitored remotely, with a little planning.

Figure 9-3 describes the basic process approach challenge for DoD program managers.

Figure 9-3 The basic process approach used in program management

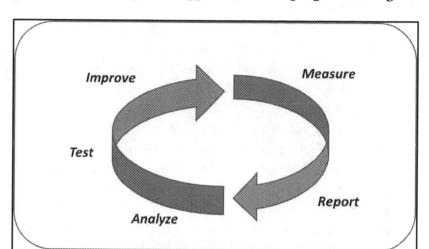

Whether you call it "Plan – Organize – Actuate – Control" as we Business majors called it in 1965; "Define – Measure – Analyze – Improve – Control (DMAIC)", if you are into Six Sigma; or "Plan – Do – Check – Act" as everybody else does, it's all the same. Your challenge *now* is that you may have to manage or audit much (if not all) of the processes from a distance.

Recovery Time Objective

The Recovery Time Objective (RTO) is the duration of time and a service level within which a program's processes must be restored after a disaster, in order to avoid unacceptable breakdowns in continuity. Often used with Information Technology (IT), RTOs can be used to measure the time it takes after the disruption to recover data.

RTOs also help to determine how long a business can survive with reduced infrastructure and services.

RTOs are often complicated. IT departments can streamline some of the recovery processes by automating them as much as possible, with tripwires and preplanned responses built into the software. A meaningful RTO involves the entire infrastructure of the organization.

Auditing – more essential than ever

An "audit" (for our purposes) is a systematic, independent, and documented process for obtaining objective evidence, and evaluating it, in order to determine the extent to which program criteria (policies, procedures, or requirements) are being fulfilled.

Many DoD contractors routinely "certify" to one or more of the International Standards Organization (ISO) Management Standards (e.g.; ISO 9001:2015: Quality Management Systems). Not only are those organizations subject to periodic audits by accredited certification bodies, but have an obligation to internally *audit themselves* in order to ensure compliance with the International Standard and maintain their certifications. Adherence to the International Standards also indirectly audits contractors to the requirements of the DoD contract.

Accordingly, program managers for these "ISO-Certified" DoD contractors have at their disposal the ability to: (1) directly audit the contractor; (2) directly assess the contractor's ability to audit itself; and (3) monitor the status of the contractors' certifications.

More than any other meaningful assessment, audits can be conducted and monitored remotely. Additionally, remote audits take less time to schedule and conduct. Remote audits eliminate budget-busting "other direct costs" such as airline tickets, hotel rooms, meals, and rental cars. Findings, feedback, and corrective actions may be faster as well, especially when working with decentralized or overseas operations or organizations.

Forward-looking certification registrars and management consultants of my acquaintance add value by offering new and existing clients *remote* audits; wherein they optimize document reviews via emails; conduct ZOOM and SKYPE conferences and interviews, and critiques; and (last but not least) use telephone cameras to remotely observe factory floors, warehouses, and loading docks.

Tabletop exercises and TACSITS

> **Tabletop exercises can be pandemic "rehearsals"**

A tabletop exercise is an activity in which key personnel assigned high-level operational and administrative roles and responsibilities gather to deliberate various simulated emergency or rapid response situations. Tabletops are used frequently to improve team responses, disaster preparedness, and emergency planning; and also contribute lessons learned to less time-critical challenges, like stateside program administration. Tabletop exercises can serve as "disruption rehearsals" by simulating actual events for preparation before, progress during, and recovery after, the simulated disruption.

Tactical Situations (TACSITS) are scenarios based on real-world conditions used to shape and forecast future operations. They give structure, substance, and direction to tabletop exercises. Computer modeling and simulation are used when insufficient data or knowledge exists. Figure 9-4 describes the creation and continuing improvement of TACSITS.

Figure 9-4 Developing a Pandemic TACSIT

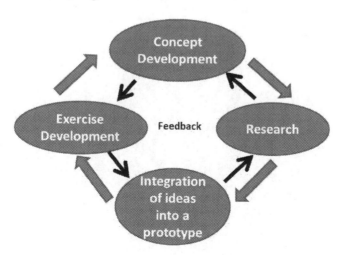

An enduring feedback loop increases productivity and potential contribution. The more remote the operation – the greater the need for real-time feedback.

A pandemic TACSIT can be as useful as TACSIT developed for a more traditional warfighting missions, such as a SEAL incursion, cargo routing, or noncombatant evacuation.

SUMMARY

The COVID 19 Pandemic underscored the need for continuity plans and the decisions that they include; decisions that must be the product of formal, structured, and defensible processes. Otherwise, they will be as meaningless and potentially dangerous as an empty fire extinguisher.

Compliance without Continuity is meaningless, in even the most benign scenarios. Disruptions and disasters like the COVID 19 Pandemic can destroy a DoD program from all sides simultaneously.

Continuity means the ability to deliver previously agreed products and services even under extremely negative situations, such as a pandemic. Continuity plans, made up of tripwires and preplanned responses guide organizations during and after disruptive events, to speed up immediate response, recovery, and resumption of minimum operational conditions, and restoration of normal operations.

Continuity requires the same best management practices that program managers already use in every contract, program, or process; but with a greatly enhanced wariness for the unexpected. See table 7-1.

Audits, internal or external, remote or on-site, are the essence of compliance monitoring, feedback, corrective action, and continual improvement.

Tabletop exercises and TACSITS can be excellent "disruption rehearsals." They can simulate actual events for preparation before, progress during, and recovery after a disruptive event.

The Program Manager's challenge *today* is to manage many (if not all) of the programs from a distance. The good news is that most good management practices can be managed and monitored remotely, and are already being monitored remotely for decentralized and overseas organizations.

If it helps in the development of a sense of urgency for continuity planning: think of COVID19 as a "bio-weapon," employed by a formidable adversary who is intent on world domination. In fact, I highly recommend it.

CHAPTER TEN

Contingency Planning

Organizations need to make security one of their key missions, and then approach it like any other: establish policies and procedures, identify threats, conduct risk assessments, implement processes, identify corrective actions, and establish a mindset of continuous improvement. And audit.

This chapter and those that follow will highlight specific topics, in the hope that they will inspire managers to create and maintain robust organizational security programs and operate them as any other indispensable business function. It discusses Contingency Planning and why it is an essential part of any organization or mission

Check Points

- ✓ Security-minded organizations need to establish, implement, and maintain appropriate plans and procedures (e.g., backing up of records or files) for responses to security incidents and emergency situations, and to prevent and/or mitigate the likely consequences associated with them.
- ✓ Emergency response may be thought of as conducting normal business processes operations at faster-than-normal speeds. It follows, therefore, that normal processes must be compatible (if not identical in many respects) with emergency operations.
- ✓ Emergency response plans and procedures should include all information dealing with identified facilities or services that may be required during or after incidents, disruptions, or emergency situations, in order to restore continuity of operations.

✓ Organizations should periodically review the effectiveness of their emergency preparedness, response, and recovery plans and procedures, especially after the occurrence of incidents or emergency situations caused by security breaches and/or threats.

✓ Security-minded managers and auditors will test these procedures periodically (as applicable), including scheduling drills and exercises and developing lessons learned and corrective actions as appropriate.

1. **What is Contingency Planning and where does it fit?**

Here is a practical definition for Contingency Planning from an excellent book:

> *"The process of planning for response to an event or emergency, managing the escalation of an emergency into a crisis condition, recovery and resumption of activities from an emergency or crisis for the infrastructure, critical processes, and other elements of a business or organization. The process of building all the elements of a plan focused on mitigating any interruption to business operations."*[22]

As figure 10-1 implies, thorough contingency planning requires:

- The identification of every aspect and requirement of the organization – all missions and under both normal and emergency operations;

- Continuous feedback between the planning and execution of those normal and emergency operations;

- The establishment of goals, objectives, metrics, and measures of effectiveness (MOE) with which to assess the feedback, and identify/analyze gaps between the actual and the required;

- Systems of controls for processing the results of the gap identification and analyses; and

- A Continuous Improvement *imperative* and mindset to motivate and optimize the entire process.

---

[22] Halibozek, E. et al, *The Corporate Security Professional's Handbook on Terrorism*, Butterworth-Heinemann, Burlington, MA, 2008

Figure 10-1 Contingency Planning Content

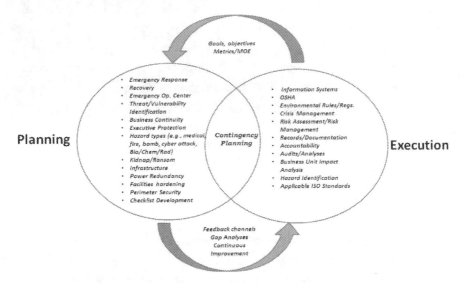

You might think that contingency planning strongly resembles regular organizational planning. You would be right.

2. Contingency Planning and Contingency Plans – Not the same

Much has been written about the difference between the process of "planning" and the creation of "plans." Some of our greatest Military thinkers have praised the process of planning and condemned the creation of arsenals of "plans".[23]

Even the most thoughtfully developed plans often fall short in their implementation because they either:

- Never get fully disseminated; or
- Cannot be executed by on-scene management; or
- Leave out critical considerations; or
- Require injections of specialized training; or
- Never get exercised, and (accordingly) never get adjusted; or

---

[23] Patton and Eisenhower were two – nice to know that they agreed on something.

- Never get updated to reflect new procedures or capital improvements; or
- Were plagiarized from a similar but separate organization.

The list could go on, but you get the idea.

If a required course of action is contained within a current plan (i.e., it was anticipated), the current plan survives intact. However, if the required course of action is (in some manner) beyond the current plan, *re-planning* is necessary, which wastes time and manpower and degrades mission effectiveness.

All plans need to have built-in "tripwires" or "pre-planned responses," that allow on-scene managers to *execute* when they are satisfied that pre-determined criteria have been met. Timeliness of execution should be incorporated into the strategy and structure of any plan. However, if the *decision* to execute requires the staffing, concurrence, and/or permission of higher authority, that timeliness can be diminished or even lost completely.

The Military helped solve the problem of too many plans and not enough planning, and of "execution by committee" with the concept of *Situational Awareness*, or the ability to recognize a situation (or a change in a situation) identify and assess the options, select a course of action, AND translate it into *actionable* orders. For the rest of us, civilian organizations maintain situational awareness when they share, internally and externally, the same operational (big) picture; and deviations or fluctuations are recognized more rapidly by managers, who can implement corrective actions almost spontaneously. Managers and auditors should look for and encourage situational awareness when they look at the *feedback, communication,* and *continuous improvement* mechanisms in the organization.

Other, more specific opportunities for Management to incorporate situational awareness can be found in:

- Standard operating procedures or SOPs
- Information management (including weather prediction)
- Report generation and simplification
- Pre-planned responses
- Alarm and alert systems
- Training and qualification systems

- Executive "dashboards."
- Clear-cut lines of authority (everybody knows who's in charge; and local managers have sufficient authority to initiate and support expedient recovery).

Top Management needs to focus on this last bullet. The ability of an on-scene manager to enter into contracts or to purchase needed goods and services unilaterally is, in my experience, absolutely essential during contingency operations.

> *Several years ago, while working as a Military Analyst, I helped to reconstruct contingency response command and control at major U.S. Navy shore installations on the Gulf Coast before, during, and after hurricanes Katrina, Rita, and Wilma. The analysis confirmed (to nobody's surprise) the following with regard to contingency planning and situational awareness:*
>
> 1. *Installation commanders and staffs had prepared documented contingency plans and situational awareness strategies from which to execute flexible responses. Once vital services were restored on-base, the Military went into the local communities to help. Local governments and FEMA lacked the required preparation, training, and expertise.*
> 2. *Those same installation commanders had conducted exercises, gathered feedback and "lessons learned" and honed their future responses long before onset of those hurricanes. Local governments and FEMA had not.*
> 3. *Local governments turned to the Military not only to restore utilities (e.g., providing emergency power to local hospitals and cell phone towers) but to set up command centers in the cities and "assist" local officials through recovery and restoration.*

> 4. *FEMA routinely usurped power and took over direction of local emergency operations. FEMA should never have tried, for example, to tell Naval air station commanders how to conduct flight operations or tell (U.S. Coast Guard) port captains how to conduct search and rescue operations.*

Figure 10-2 describes the Contingency Plan "continuum. That is, the path from and back to normal operations after a disruptive incident. The path takes the organization through Response, Continuity, Recovery/Resumption, and back to Normal. The ability of the organization to travel safely and expeditiously along this path depends on the suitability and robustness of the planning, the consistency and likeness of normal and contingency operations, and the ability of on-scene personnel to react without the need for further guidance and direction from above.

Figure 10-2 The Contingency Plan Continuum

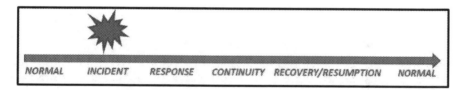

NORMAL   INCIDENT   RESPONSE   CONTINUITY   RECOVERY/RESUMPTION   NORMAL

Contingency planning, according to *NFPA 1600* consists of five components:

1. The Strategic Plan
2. The Emergency Operations/Response Plan
3. The Mitigation Plan
4. The Recovery Plan
5. The Continuity Plan.

However, the possible establishment of five separate plans (possibly created by five separate levels or functions) creates numerous real and potential interoperability complications, especially over time, as some activities change and others do not. The "Strategic Plan" required is actually a subset of the overall strategic plan governing the organization. With that in mind, a more streamlined contingency planning strategy (see figure 10-3) would likely be more executable.

Figure 10-3 Evolving the Contingency Plan

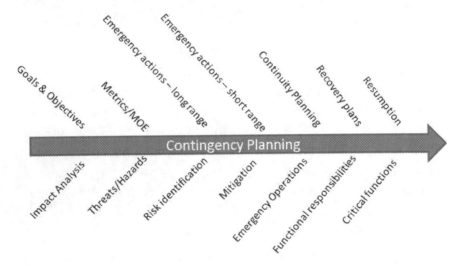

All the components of the diagram must be combined, revised, and combined again to create operating plans for normal operations anyway. The shift to a contingency scenario should be as automatic and transparent as possible.

3. Executing Contingency Planning (aka Emergency Response)

As discussed, organizations must be capable of *executing* contingency plans – quickly, efficiently, and completely, and contingency operations should be *as close as possible to normal operations*, especially since the goal of contingency operations is the rapid restoration of normal operations. Accordingly, contingency operations should support normal operations and (just like normal operations) should reflect the following:

- Total asset visibility throughout the supply chain
- Organic self-auditing and data collection and analysis

- Process mapping and balancing
- Restoration goals (e.g., pieces/hour after 24 hours)
- Clearly defined lines of authority and responsibility
- Up-to-date threat, vulnerability, needs, and risk assessments
- Personnel qualifications, based on needs assessments
- Acquisition authority of on-site management.
- Exercises that generate lessons learned and feedback.

Exercises should include the involvement and participation of local authorities, or they will risk communications and interoperability problems when the real thing happens. The involvement of the local authorities of host nations (when doing business outside the U.S.) is even more important. By way of example, commercial ships entering foreign or domestic ports are required to have "port security plans" that mesh with the security plans of the ports, in order that the actions of both ship and port support and complement each other. Responses are automatic and unilateral and each player knows what to expect from the other.

Organizations can both enhance and expedite their preparations for exercise or actual contingencies by conducting informal "table top" exercises, during which representatives from involved organizations come together to "game" potential contingencies. They develop cooperative reactions to imposed threat scenarios. Table top exercises can be quick, inexpensive, vehicles to identify and assess threats, develop needs and risk assessments, and prioritize allocation of personnel and funding. The results of a structured table top exercise can become very meaningful audit findings.

4. Continuity and Recovery – Back to (a "New") Normal as Quickly as Possible

Many auditors witness (and often pass judgment on) the exercise of authority, responsibility, and accountability by Top Management. We audit quality, environmental compliance, supply chain security, and the like. We look at sales, profit and loss, and training – all in the context of *how* the organization should operate. Accordingly, we can lose sight of the fact that Top Management has (as its most fundamental duty) the responsibility for maintaining the ability of the organization *to operate,* and to operate without disruption. That is, the ability to maintain "continuity".

British Standard 25999 defines *business continuity* as "the strategic and tactical capability of the organization to plan for and respond to incidents and business disruptions in order to continue business operations at an acceptable pre-defined level;" and *business continuity management* as "a holistic management process that identifies potential threats to an organization and the impacts to business operations that those threats, if realized, might cause, and which provides a framework for building organizational resilience with the capability for an effective response that safeguards the interests of its key stakeholders, reputation, brand, and value creating activities."

Recoveries are measured not in terms of days or hours, but rather in terms of re-establishments or re-achievements of previously defined objectives. For example:

- The resumption of product or service delivery after an incident; or
- The resumption of performance of an activity or service after an incident; or
- The recovery of an IT system or software after an incident.

Again, there must be genuine commonality and cohesion of structure, processes, and lines of authority for an organization to move from normal to emergency, contingency, continuity, to recovery and (back) to normal operations. However, Management should have as its recovery goal, the establishment of a "new" normal. That is, come back from the contingency stronger or better. Chapter Nine has more on this.

5. To Plan or not to Plan – There is no Question

Many of us, in our auditing adventures, have met managers who consider contingency planning unnecessary. Their reasons vary, but when they directly or indirectly discourage contingency planning, they deny their organizations an *adhesive* that more fully bonds their people and processes together, through the identification and protection of all products and services, risks and rewards, lines of authority, responsibility, and feedback. Additionally:

- An incident management capability is enabled for effective response
- Critical activities are identified
- Acceptable (and unacceptable) levels of risk are identified as a function of threat and impact analysis
- Information flows are enabled, reinforced, or terminated as a function of Confidentiality, Integrity, Availability, Currency, and Expedience.
- The interaction of the organization with regulators, communities, governments, and (possibly) host nations is developed, documented, and understood
- Personnel are trained to respond quickly, meaningfully, and *safely* to incidents or disruptions – natural or man-made
- Key lines of authority, communication, and supply/resupply are reinforced and secured
- Resources are identified, prioritized, and programmed
- Regulatory compliance responsibilities are understood
- Stakeholders understand their duties in direct or indirect support of the organization
- The organization's reputation is protected and (most likely) enhanced.

SUMMARY

All organizations are subject to incidents and disruptions of operations. Disruptions can be the result of terrorist or cyber-attack, natural disasters such as hurricanes, earthquakes, or floods, or internal occurrences such as fires, utility outages, hacking, or HAZMAT spills. Managers and auditors must develop and refine the ability of organizations to react to the emergency, mitigate it, and initiate restorations until normal operations are fully resumed – all while protecting the welfare and safety of their personnel and the community.

Contingency planning and all that goes with it should be considered not as a cosmetic or mandated expenditure of time and funding, but as an extension of normal management processes – one that adds great value to the organization.

Good managers can do it – good auditors can help.

CHAPTER ELEVEN

Business Impact Analysis

Organizations need to make *Security* one of their key missions, and then approach it like any other: establish policies and procedures, identify threats, conduct risk assessments, implement processes, identify corrective actions, train key people, and establish a mindset of continuous improvement. And audit.

Chapter Six discussed Contingency Planning as a vital function that managers must perform and auditors must verify. I urge readers to embrace their principles and practices.

It is my hope that managers will to create, maintain, and continually improve robust organizational security programs and run them on a daily basis, as any other indispensable business function.

Points to Remember

- ✓ The impact of a natural or man-made incident to an organization can be minor, major, or disastrous, depending on the organization's ability to foresee that incident, defend the organization from it, and mitigate its effects as quickly and safely as possible.
- ✓ Impacts may involve loss of assets, loss of income, loss of clients, or loss of life, and almost certainly damage to the organization's strategy, products or services, and (possibly) its reputation.
- ✓ Business Impact Analysis (BIA) enables organizations to recognize what needs to be done *before* an incident occurs, in order that it may manage its way through consequences without unacceptable

losses or delays, and restore normal operations as soon as possible. It is a necessary sub-set of an organization's risk management program and helps enable the organization to measure impacts in terms of finance and operations.

✓ Management must perform BIA on an ongoing basis; auditors can help.

What is Business Impact Analysis and where does it fit?

Figure 11-1 describes the contingency "continuum, updated from earlier. It is the route away from and back to normal operations after a disruptive incident. The route takes the organization through Response, Continuity, Recovery/Resumption, and back to Normal. The ability of the organization to maneuver safely and expeditiously along this path depends on the suitability and robustness of the planning, the consistency and likeness of normal and contingency operations, and the ability of on-scene personnel to react without the need for further guidance and direction from above.

Figure 11-1 The Contingency Continuum

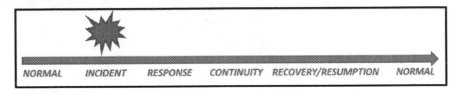

NORMAL   INCIDENT   RESPONSE   CONTINUITY   RECOVERY/RESUMPTION   NORMAL

Managers and auditors recognize the necessity of risk assessment in everyday operations. Like risk assessment, BIA is an essential part of the (pre-incident) planning process. It is where Management identifies, as best it can, the financial and operational impact of an interruption of its activities. BIA should be thought of as a logical and necessary component of the overall Risk Management Strategy, as shown in table 11-1.

Table11-1 Elements of the Risk Assessment/Business Impact Analysis

Required Activity	Risk Assessment	BIA
Threat identification	X	X
Critical activities identification	X	X
Interoperability/Interdependency	X	X
Vulnerabilities	X	X
Critical Infrastructure	X	X
Facilities/Resources	X	X
Human factors	X	X
State of training	X	X
Controls/mitigations	X	X

Singly or together, both risk assessment and business impact analysis should consistently identify and assess impacts to the organization if assets are damaged or destroyed, or capabilities are in some way denied.

2. Identification of critical activities and interdependencies

A quick, initial, way to identify critical activities is to list every activity of the organization and categorize each in terms of whether its disruption/ suspension would:

- Constitute a minor emergency; or
- Constitute a major emergency; or
- Constitute a disaster.

Table 11-2 describes a simple way to display this process.

Table 11-2 Assessing the loss of normal activities (example)

Normal Activity (Suspended/disrupted)	Minor	Major	Disaster
Billing	X		
Shipping		X	
Receiving			X
Processing			X
Inventory Management	X		
Required Utilities			X
Ground Transportation		X	
Air Transportation	X		
Intranet		X	
Internet			X

"Downtimes" are essential considerations, since many activities, if denied for a short period of time, constitute only minor problems. However, if those same activities are denied for extended periods, resultant problems could be major, or even disastrous. Similarly, BIA must include thorough examination of the *vulnerability* of the assets themselves. For example, older buildings without back-up emergency power, suppression, or sprinkler systems may be more vulnerable to natural or man-made threats than newer, more modern facilities.

The *interdependence* of activities and operations is also an essential part of the BIA. For example, an asset (e.g., the intranet) may be "off-line" for three days before it becomes (in and of itself) problematic. However, interdependent processes (e.g. inventory management or shipping) may be impacted sooner and more acutely.

Threat assessment, prioritization, and risk acceptance

Threats (or "hazards") to an organization's unrestricted operations can come in many forms, and, depending on those operations, can have major consequences over long and short durations.

Making a matrix like figure 11- 2 is a quick method of both identifying and assessing the threats and expressing them as risks to the organization.

Figure 11-2 A basic risk assessment matrix

SECURITY TASKS	Terrorist Attack	Utility Loss	Hacker Cyber Attack	Industrial Espionage	Strike	Agent Spill	Natural Disaster	Related reporting	Total	Average
1. Security / Surveillance										
Detecting/Identifying unauthorized movement - personnel	9	4	9	9	3	5	8	8	55	7
Detecting/Identifying unauthorized movement - vehicles	9	4	9	9	3	5	8	8	55	7
Surveillance of restricted areas	4	4	9	9	3	5	8	8	50	6
Securing incident sites	9	9	9	5	3	5	8	8	56	7
Detection of unauthorized material	9	4	9	5	6	5	8	8	54	7
Surveillance of facility access points	9	4	6	5	6	5	8	8	51	6
Harbor surveillance	6	4	6	5	3	5	8	8	45	6
Automatic security systems	4	4	6	5	3	5	8	8	43	5

Table 11-3 contains some of the threats that I use when helping organizations to form security risk management strategies and models. Numerical values (1-10) are assigned to each, and then averages are taken.

116

Table 11-3 Step One – Threat identification and assessment

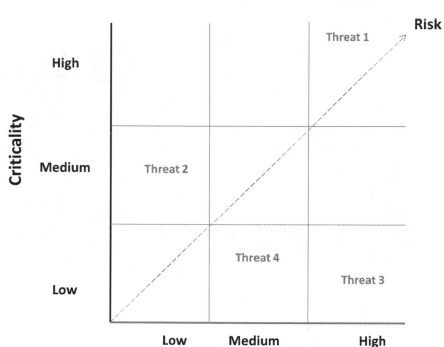

These tables are not all-inclusive or appropriate for all organizations. Threat lists should be developed and modified to fit the needs and conditions of the specific organizations[24]

Numerical values are assigned to each threat and its associated criticality and vulnerability (e.g., to a mission or operation) according to the formula:

> ### *Risk = Threat x Criticality x Vulnerability*

---

[24] I cover Risk Management extensively in my book: *Fixes That Last – The Executive's Guide to Fix It or Lose It Management.*

Figure 11-3 shows the final risk picture

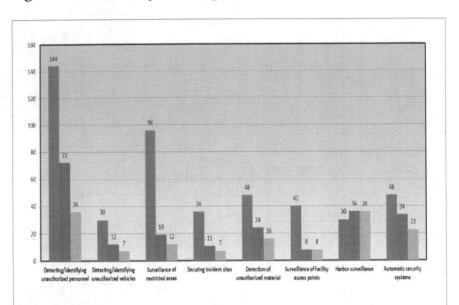

Risk Management is an essential component of three popular and valuable International Standards. These exceptionally useful ISO Standards, as quoted below, require organizations to identify and assess threats and their associated risks[25].

ISO 14000 (Environmental Management Systems)

Clause 4.3.1 Environmental Aspects
"The organization shall establish, implement, and maintain a procedure:

a) To <u>identify the environmental aspects</u> *of its activities, products, and services within the defined scope of the environmental management system that it can control and those that it can influence taking into account planned or new developments, or new or modified activities, products, or services; and*

b) To <u>determine those aspects that have or can have a significant impact on the environment</u> *(i.e. significant environmental aspects)."*

---

[25] Underlining added for effect.

ISO 9000 (Quality Management Systems)

Clause 5.1 Management Commitment

"Top *management shall provide evidence of its commitment to the development of the quality management system and <u>continually improving its effectiveness</u>* by:

a) *Communicating to the organization the importance of <u>meeting customer as well as statutory and regulatory requirements</u>*
b) *Establishing a quality policy*
c) <u>*Ensuring quality objectives are established*</u>
d) <u>*Conducting management reviews,*</u> *and*
e) *Ensuring the availability of resources."*

ISO 27000 (Information Security Management Systems)

Clause 4.2.2 Implement and operate the ISMS

The organization shall …formulate a risk treatment plan that identifies the appropriate management action, resources, responsibilities, and priorities for managing information security risks.

ISO 28000: (Security Management Systems for the Supply Chain)

Clause 4.3.1 Security Risk Assessment

"*The organization shall establish and maintain procedures for the ongoing <u>identification and assessment of security threats and security management-related threats and risks, and the identification and implementation of necessary management control measures</u>. Security threats and risk identification, assessment, and control methods should, as a minimum, be <u>appropriate to the measure and scale of the operations</u>. This assessment should consider the likelihood of an event and all of its consequences which shall include……"*

Doing risk management on a spreadsheet customized for a specific organization can provide Management with a fast, descriptive tool to:

•   Standardize, assess, prioritize, and display readiness for specific business or mission scenarios

119

- Predict the impact of personnel and material changes before time or funds are expended
- Create uniform reports to higher authority
- Predict readiness by assessing risks. (See Chapter one)

Functions (e.g., sums, multiplications, averages) can be programmed into the spreadsheet, and graphs can be created automatically as values are introduced or changed.

An organization certified to one or more of those Standards is already well on the way to effective BIA. Organizations can easily add BIA components to their existing (ISO-certified) Risk Management program.

Incident or event (post) analysis and evaluation

Incidents or events that have, in fact, caused damage or disruption should be evaluated as thoroughly as possible, as a method of validating or updating existing BIA strategies and assessments. It is vital after an incident to determine which pre-planned strategies, procedures, and/or mitigations worked and which fell short of expectations.

Analyses must determine the extent of any (real or potential) damage and the potential for subsequent damage or disruption. This is also where Management establishes or modifies its priorities for restoration of impacted processes, technologies, and infrastructure. There will be more on that when we discuss *Business Continuity Management*.

Natural and man-made incident impacts – you can prepare for both at the same time

> *Military folks know that you don't track terrorist attacks for 4-7 days on The Weather Channel.*

When organizations (Military or civilian) prepare for natural disasters, they are (whether they realize it or not) hardening themselves against man-made incidents as well. The similarity of incident impacts is summarized in table 11-4.

Table 11-4 Common impacts of natural and man-made incidents

Incident Impact	Natural	Man Made
Loss of utilities (including power and sewage treatment)	X	X
Loss of connectivity and situational awareness (e.g., internet, and/or cell phone towers)	X	X
Personnel casualties and MEDEVAC	X	X
Loss of drinking water, HVAC	X	X
Personnel evacuation	X	X
Loss of movement and transportation	X	X
Isolation of areas or facilities	X	X
Loss of on site authority, command and control	X	X

So then, you say: "Do I prepare for man-made incidents **only** by preparing for natural disasters?" Let me answer this way: Military folks know that you don't get to track a terrorist attack for 4-7 days on *The Weather Channel*.

Auditing Business Impact

Alright then, we have covered the importance of assessing the real or potential impact of natural and man-made incidents, and how important it is for managers to use BIA to help to ensure safe and secure operations. Now, how do we, as auditors, help managers to do BIA effectively? We do what we do best: we audit. Here, are some general areas of BIA where, I believe, auditors can do the greatest good for their client organizations.

A. General BIA Requirements

1. Does the organization have a BIA Plan and does it determine and document the impact of a disruption to its key activities and operations, to include:

   a. Key products and services

   b. Data collection and key performance indicators

   c. Identification of all stakeholders

   d. Standard and emergency operating procedures

   e. A risk management process and strategy that in which all threats, criticalities, and vulnerabilities are identified

   f. Sharing of all communications and plans at all levels

g. Subsequent impacts that may occur over time

h. Maximum tolerable periods of disruption

i. Minimal levels of recovery

j. Expected time before normal operations can resume

k. Critical interdependencies

l. Supporting infrastructure

m. Supplier and sub-contractor responsibilities

n. Restoration priorities

o. Post-event evaluation (exercise and real-world)?

2. Are all activities identified and categorized by whether their disruption or loss would result in:

a. Minor disruption of operations

b. Major disruption of operations

c. Disastrous consequences?

3. Does the Business Impact Analysis include:

a. Personnel and the public

b. Normal and emergency communications – internal and external

c. Damage or loss of property, technology, or information

d. Statutory and regulatory requirements and the ability to meet them fully

e. The organization's reputation and goodwill

f. The environment and ecosystems

g. Community responsibilities

h. Conduits for timely feedback?

B. Personnel training and qualification

1. Are key training and qualification needs and competencies identified?

2. Are training resources adequate for internal training needs?

3. Are all personnel trained in organization-specific technologies as appropriate?

4. Are personnel training records maintained, and do they include:

   a. Education
   b. Experience
   c. Training
   d. Qualifications?

5. Do personnel understand the relevance and importance of what they do and how they contribute to the continuity of the organization in the event of an incident or disruption?

6. Does the organization evaluate the effectiveness of the training provided?

7. Does the organization define "competency" and how personnel can demonstrate competency with regard to organizational security?

C. Self-Assessment and Continual Improvement

1. Does the organization have Internal Audit procedures and do they:

   a. Conform to the requirements of the International Standard and relevant legislation or regulations;
   b. Conform to the identified information security requirements;
   c. Are effectively implemented and maintained; and
   d. Perform as expected?

2. Are all security - related processes and procedures audited at least once per year?

3. Does the organization continually improve the effectiveness of its BIA through the use of:

   a. Policy and objectives
   b. Audit results
   c. Analysis of data
   d. Corrective and preventive actions
   e. Management review?

SUMMARY

All organizations are subject to incidents and disruptions of operations resulting from terrorist or cyber-attack, natural disasters such as hurricanes, earthquakes, or floods, or internal occurrences such as fires, utility outages, hacking, or HAZMAT spills.

Business Impact Analysis, when merged with an organization's overall Risk Management strategy, identifies and quantifies potential threats in terms of operational and financial consequences. More importantly, BIA helps Management to predict and prepare for incidents, and in doing so, mitigate or minimize them.

CHAPTER TWELVE

Business Continuity Management

Organizations need to make Security a key mission, and then approach it like any other: establish policies and procedures, identify threats, conduct risk assessments, implement processes, identify corrective actions, train/ qualify key people, and establish a mindset of continuous improvement. And audit.

It is my hope that managers and auditors will to want create, maintain, and continually improve robust organizational security programs and track them on a daily basis, as they would with any other indispensable business function.

Points to Remember

- ✓ The impact of a natural or man-made incident to an organization can be minor, major, or disastrous, depending on not only the magnitude of the incident, but also on the organization's ability to anticipate that incident, defend the organization from it, and mitigate its effects as quickly and safely as possible.
- ✓ Impacts may involve loss of assets, loss of income, loss of clients, or loss of life, and almost certainly damage to the organization's strategy, products or services, and (last but not leased) its reputation.
- ✓ Business Impact Analysis (BIA) enables organizations to recognize what needs to be done *before* an incident occurs, in order that it may manage its way through consequences without unacceptable losses or delays, and restore normal operations as soon as possible. It is a necessary sub-set of an organization's risk management

program and helps to enable the organization to measure impacts in terms of finance and operations.

✓ With the potential impacts identified and assessed, Management must then act to eliminate or mitigate those impacts in a way that restores continuity of operations to an acceptable level, moving the organization to the ultimate goal of complete recovery and resumption of normal operations.

1. What is Business Continuity Management?

Figure 12-1 revises the contingency continuum. It traces the route away from and back to normal operations after a disruptive incident. The route takes the organization through Response, Continuity, Recovery/Resumption, and back to Normal. Again, the ability of the organization to maneuver safely and expeditiously along this path depends on the suitability and robustness of the planning, the consistency and likeness of normal and contingency operations, and the ability of on-scene personnel to react without the need for further guidance and direction from higher authority.

Figure 12-1 The Contingency Continuum

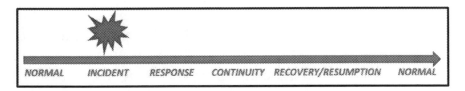

NORMAL   INCIDENT   RESPONSE   CONTINUITY   RECOVERY/RESUMPTION   NORMAL

BS 25999 describes Business Continuity Management or BCM as a "holistic management process that identifies potential threats to and organization and the impacts to business operations that those threats, might cause, and which provides a framework for building organizational resilience with the capability for an effective response that safeguards the interests of key stakeholders, reputation, brand, and value-creating activities." [26]

---

[26] "BS" stands for *British Standard* – at least in this instance. Actually, BS 25999 provides an excellent template for effective BCM creation and maintenance.

2. Determining BCM Requirements

Each office/site in the organization should estimate the resources that it will require upon resumption of activities. These include:

a) Staff resources, including numbers, skills, and knowledge requirements
b) The work site(s) and facilities required
c) Supporting technology and equipment
d) Provision of information, including previous work and work currently in progress, sufficiently up-to-date and accurate to allow activities to continue effectively at the agreed level
e) External suppliers and services.

3. Resource Requirements

The resources required for business continuity and business recovery include:

a) Security
b) Transportation logistics
c) Welfare needs
d) Emergency expenses
e) Premises
f) Technology, including communications
g) Information which may include:
1) Financial details (e.g., payroll)
2) Customer account records
3) Supplier and stakeholder details
4) Legal documents
5) Other services documents and agreements
6) Supplies
7) Management of, and communication with, stakeholders.

4. Incident Response & Business Continuity Management Planning

Titles like "emergency planning", "continuity planning," and "contingency planning" are often used interchangeably. Each title is only meaningful when defined in terms of the organization to which its measures are being applied. Measures applied in support of BCM should be never be considered as cosmetic or externally mandated expenditures of time and funding, but rather as extensions of normal management processes – extensions that add great value to the organization, its mission, and its processes.

Emergency responses may be thought of as normal operations at faster-than-normal speeds, or they may mean something entirely different. The security-minded organization needs to establish, implement, and maintain appropriate plans and procedures (e.g., backing up of records or files) for responses to security incidents and emergency situations, and to prevent and/or mitigate the likely consequences associated with them. Emergency plans and procedures should include all information dealing with identified facilities or services that may be affected during or after incidents or emergency situations, in order to reestablish continuity of operations.

Figure 12-2 contains the many component parts of the BCM process. It is really not important to think of these parts in terms of what titles under which they belong. That will likely differ with every organization and management approach. It is only important to consider all of them in the overall strategy.

Figure 12-2 The Incident Response and Business Continuity Management Process

Goals, objectives
Metrics/MOE

- Emergency Response
- Recovery
- Emergency Op. Center
- Threat/Vulnerability
  Identification
- Business Continuity
- Executive Protection
- Hazard types (e.g., medical, fire, bomb, cyber attack, Bio/Chem/Rad)
- Kidnap/Ransom
- Infrastructure
- Power Redundancy
- Facilities hardening
- Perimeter Security
- Checklist Development

Emergency Response & Continuity Planning

- Information Systems
- OSHA
- Environmental Rules/Regs.
- Crisis Management
- Risk Assessment/Risk Management
- Records/Documentation
- Accountability
- Audits/Analyses
- Business Unit Impact Analysis
- Hazard Identification
- Applicable ISO Standards

Feedback channels
Gap Analyses
Continuous
Improvement

Planning

Execution

No organization is exempt from incidents or disruptions to operations. Disruptions can be the result of terrorist or cyber-attacks, natural disasters such as hurricanes, earthquakes, or floods, or internal occurrences such as fires, utility outages, hacking, or HAZMAT spills.

Managers and auditors must develop and refine the ability of organizations to react to the emergency, mitigate it, and initiate restorations until normal operations are fully resumed – all while protecting the welfare and safety of their personnel and the community.

5. Operating Procedures

The Incident Response and Business Continuity Management Plan, as modified for each of an organization's sites, should include operating procedures, with flowcharts, checklists, and pre-planned responses needed to manage the immediate consequences of a business disruption, in order to:

a) Ensure that individual safety remains paramount throughout recovery and restoration
b) Reflect the results of a Risk Management and Business Impact Analysis strategy
c) Structure strategic and tactical options for rapid execution
d) Prevent further or subsequent loss or unavailability of critical activities
e) Support remaining resources.

6. Incident Response plans/task lists

Each site should maintain a response plan and task list containing:

a) Structured checklists of prioritized actions to be taken to assess/restore continuity
b) The personnel responsible for executing the responses
c) The procedure to be used for rendering decisions on site
d) Personnel to be consulted before emergency actions are executed
e) Personnel to be consulted after incident response are executed
f) Personnel assignments
g) Mobilization of external resources
h) Communication plans
i) Manual workarounds (if required) for system recovery.

7. The Business Continuity Management Plan

The Business Continuity Plan (BCMP) enables an organization to recover or maintain its activities in the event of a disruption to normal business operations. It is implemented to support critical activities required in support of the organization's missions in the event of an incident. Elements of the Plan may be activated wholly or in part at any stage of the response to the incident. Figure 12-3 describes the inter-dependent nature of the BCMP.

Figure 12-3 Business Continuity Management Planning

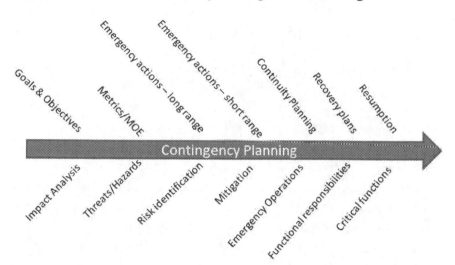

Organizations should periodically review the effectiveness of their emergency preparedness, response, and recovery plans and procedures, especially after the occurrence of incidents or emergency situations caused by security breaches and threats. Security-minded managers and auditors will "test" or "game" these procedures periodically (as applicable), including scheduling drills and exercises and developing corrective actions as appropriate.

8. Recovery and resumption of operations

This topic will be covered fully in the final chapter. However, it is important at this point to remember that recoveries are measured NOT in terms of days or hours, but rather in terms of *re-establishments* or *re-achievements* of previously defined objectives. For example:

a) The resumption of product or service delivery after an incident; or
b) The resumption of performance of an activity or service after an incident; or
c) The recovery of an IT system or software after an incident.

Appendix I is a checklist that has served my clients well as they add more structure to their organizations. They are not applicable to every organization, but you'll get the idea.

9. Tactical Operations Center (TOC)

Many readers may think that a term like *tactical operations center* sounds more military than civilian. They are correct – it started with the Military. However, natural or man-made disasters (as discussed earlier) can force a headquarters to relocate its intelligence collection and its decision-making capability away from (or close to) the site of the disaster. It will not be too hard, when reviewing the two checklists below, to see their applicability to the civilian organizations that you audit.

Here again, there is no reason why civilian managers and auditors cannot look at this checklist and see many areas consistent with and appropriate for, their facilities and operations.

SUMMARY

All organizations are subject to incidents and disruptions of operations. Disruptions can be the result of terrorist or cyber-attack, natural disasters such as hurricanes, earthquakes, or floods, or internal occurrences such as fires, utility outages, hacking, or HAZMAT spills. Managers and auditors must develop and refine the ability of organizations to react to an emergency, mitigate it, and initiate restorations until normal operations are fully resumed – all while protecting the welfare and safety of their personnel and community.

Managers can do it – they have knowledge and the resources. Auditors can help – they have the organizational and analytical skills. However, both must recognize the importance, as well as the *ethical imperative* of taking on this effort wholeheartedly and succeeding at it.

CHAPTER THIRTEEN

Recovery and Restoration

Chapter Six discussed *Contingency Planning* as a vital function that managers must perform and auditors must verify. Chapter Seven discussed *Business Impact Analysis* (BIA), stressing its relationship to Risk Management. Chapter Eight discussed *Business Continuity Management* (BCM). This chapter discusses *Response and Recovery*. I would (again) urge managers and auditors to embrace their principles and practices.

Points to Remember/Review

- ✓ The impact of a natural or man-made incident to an organization can be minor, major, or disastrous, depending on not only the magnitude of the incident, but also on the organization's ability to anticipate that incident, defend the organization from it, and mitigate its effects as quickly and safely as possible.
- ✓ Impacts may involve loss of assets, loss of income, loss of clients, or loss of life, and almost certainly damage to the organization's strategy, products or services, and (last but not leased) its reputation.
- ✓ *Business Impact Analysis (BIA)* enables organizations to recognize what needs to be done *before* an incident occurs, in order that it may manage its way through consequences without unacceptable losses or delays, and restore normal operations as soon as possible. It is a necessary sub-set of an organization's risk management program and helps to enable the organization to measure impacts in terms of finance and operations.
- ✓ With the potential impacts identified and assessed, Management must then act to eliminate or mitigate those impacts in a way that

restores continuity of operations to an acceptable level, moving the organization to the ultimate goal of complete recovery and resumption of normal operations.

✓ A viable *Recovery* strategy is required *before* a disaster, not after
✓ Restoration's goal is a new normal – better than before by as many measurable standards as possible

1. What do we mean by Recovery and Restoration?

Figure 13-1 again revises the contingency continuum. It traces the route away from, and back to, normal operations after a disruptive incident. The route takes the organization through Response, Continuity, Recovery/Resumption, and back to Normal. Again, the ability of the organization to maneuver safely and expeditiously along this path depends on the suitability and robustness of the planning, the consistency and likeness of normal and contingency operations, and the ability of on-scene personnel to react without the need for further guidance and direction from higher authority.

Figure 13-1 The Contingency Continuum

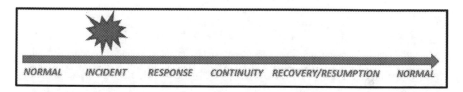

BS 25999 describes Business Continuity Management or BCM as a "holistic management process that identifies potential threats to an organization and the impacts to business operations that those threats might cause, and which provides a framework for building organizational resilience with the capability for an effective response that safeguards the interests of key stakeholders, reputation, brand, and value-creating activities." [27]

---

[27] I strongly recommend that readers obtain this Standard and become familiar with its contents. Its applications are widespread.

It is important at this point to remember that recoveries are measured NOT in terms of days or hours, but rather in terms of *re-establishments* or *re-achievements* of previously defined objectives. For example:

- The resumption of product or service delivery after an incident; or
- The resumption of performance of an activity or service after an incident; or
- The recovery of an IT system or software after an incident.

2. Recovery (Short Term, Measured Response, and Follow up)

A. *Post Event Evaluation – not your father's audit*

It is important to assess the events of an actual emergency as soon and as comprehensively as possible, in order to determine:

- Which responses and mitigations produced positive results (i.e., as planned)
- Which responses and mitigations produced negligible or no results
- Which responses and mitigations produced negative results (i.e., they actually made things worse).

Managers and auditors gain an enormously valuable source of *actionable intelligence* with the occurrence of an actual emergency. They need to maximize the collection and analysis of all data pertinent to the event. Post event evaluation (and auditing) should assess, as applicable:

- Existing emergency response plans
- Reporting procedures
- Installed communication and warning (alarm) systems
- Fire and intrusion detection alarms
- Public address systems
- Personnel assignments (e.g., floor captains)

- Network recovery and the ability to isolate, secure, and restore systems
- Coordination with local authorities
- Internal command and control
- Personnel evacuation, call-in, and reassembly
- HAZMAT creation and clean up
- Search and rescue
- After-action reports and reporting
- Adequacy/availability of pre-event threat and vulnerability assessments
- Alignment of actual events with existing risk management and strategic planning concentrations and focuses, with thought to possible revision of those concentrations and focuses
- The need for different/additional emergency training
- Social disruption (i.e., victims, evacuations, utility outages)
- The process for returning to work.

That final bullet: "the process for returning to work" is an essential inclusion to post event evaluation and a logical point from which to move on.

B. Recovery Strategy and a new "normal"

Recovery can (and should) create a <u>new normal</u>, the goal of which is higher, not lower expectations of performance and productivity.

"Recovery" is, for our purposes, the transition from disaster response back to an acceptable state of business or operational normalcy. Forward-thinking managers (and auditors) should plan on rebuilding *better*, with absolutely no thought given to settling for less or lowering the bar. Moreover, managers must have a viable recovery strategy *before* a disaster, not after. Remind yourselves of the past failings of municipal planners, who didn't start to plan recoveries until it was time to recover. A viable recovery strategy (again, planned from the beginning) can be sub-divided into <u>overlapping</u> phases, as shown in figure 13-2.

Figure 13-2 Breaking down the Recovery/Restoration phase of the Contingency Continuum

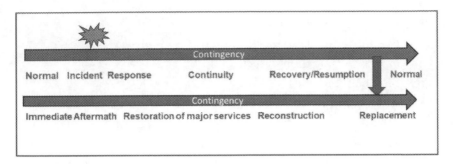

The length/duration of these four sub-phases is a function of the amount and extent of the pre-disaster planning those forward-thinking managers put into them. Recovery should be thought of as "short term" tactics, such as restoration of services, clean-up, inspections and assessments, and reestablishing interfaces. Restoration should be thought of as "long term" and involving strategies that impact the future of the community as well as that of the organization.

3. Restoration (Long Term, Sustainable, and Holistic)

Planning must focus not only on mitigating the immediate effects of disasters, but on increasing resistance to future disasters.

Managing (and auditing) *Restoration* seeks, as a goal, going beyond the status quo and using an unsolicited opportunity to measurably improve the structure, robustness, and sustainability of the (ultimately) restored organization; likewise, the community and the lives of the stakeholders. Emergency Management expert Lucien G. Canton describes Six Principles of Sustainability[28]:

1. Maintain, and if possible, enhance the quality of life
2. Enhance local economic viability
3. Promote social and intergenerational equity

---

[28] Canton, L.G, *Emergency Management, Concepts and Strategies for Effective Programs*, J. Wiley & Sons, Inc., Hoboken NJ, 2007; every organization can profit from owning a copy of this book.

4. Maintain and, if possible, enhance the quality of the environment

5. Incorporate disaster resilience and mitigation into decisions and actions

6. Use a consensus-building, participatory process when making decisions.

The planning (and auditing) described in these last four chapters must be done with the end results envisioned. Similarly, the organization's planning should be linked to the community's planning – and the *goals* of both should be the same.

4. Auditing Recovery and Restoration

Here are modified segments some of my checklists to add more structure to recovery and restoration operations and processes. If they resemble ISO checklists, it's because that where they came from.

An ISO-like approach to auditing almost always produces long term benefits, even in the short term.

A. Auditing Recovery

☐ Does the organization continually improve the effectiveness of its Recovery and Restoration strategy through the use of:

  ✓ Policy and objectives
  ✓ Audit results
  ✓ Analysis of data
  ✓ Corrective and preventive actions
  ✓ Management review?

☐ Has the organization established, implemented, and maintained appropriate plans and procedures to identify the potential for and responses to, security incidents and emergency situations, and for preventing and mitigating the likely consequences associated with them?

☐ Do the plans and procedures include maintaining information on all identified facilities or services that will be required during or after incidents or emergency situations?

☐ Does the organization periodically review the effectiveness of its emergency preparedness, response and recovery plans and procedures, in particular after the occurrence of incidents or emergency situations, and are these procedures periodically tested (as applicable)?

☐ Are training needs and competencies identified?

☐ Are training resources adequate for the internal training needs?

☐ Are all personnel trained in applicable technologies (as appropriate)?

☐ Are training records maintained?

☐ Do training records include personnel:

  o Education
  o Experience
  o Training
  o Qualifications?

☐ Do personnel understand the relevance and importance of what they do and how they contribute to the achievement of organizational goals and objectives?

☐ Does the organization evaluate the effectiveness of the training provided?

☐ Does the organization define "competency" and how personnel can demonstrate competency?

☐ Has Management identified the personnel and material resources it needs to:

  o Establish, implement, monitor, review, maintain, and improve recovery and restoration strategies;
  o Ensure that Recovery and Restoration procedures support the business requirements;
  o Identify and address legal and regulatory requirements and contractual obligations;

- o Maintain adequate organizational and personnel safety and security by correct application of all implemented controls;

- ☐ Carry out reviews when necessary, and react appropriately to the results of those reviews; and
- ☐ Does top management ensure that customer requirements are determined and are met with the aim of enhancing customer satisfaction?

B. Auditing Restoration

- ☐ Has the organization established and maintained an organizational structure of roles, responsibilities, and authorities, consistent with the achievement of its management policy, objectives, targets, and programs, and are these defined, documented, and communicated to responsible individuals?
- ☐ Does top management provide evidence of its commitment to development of the Recovery and Restoration strategies and to improving their effectiveness by:

  - o Appointing a member of top management who, irrespective of other responsibilities is responsible for the design, maintenance, documentation and improvement of Recovery and Restoration
  - o Appointing members of management with the necessary authority to ensure that the objectives and targets are implemented
  - o Identifying and monitoring the requirements and expectations of the organization's stakeholders and taking appropriate action to manage these expectations
  - o Ensuring the availability of adequate resources
  - o Communicating to the organization the importance of meeting its recovery management requirements in order to comply with its policy

- o Ensuring any programs generated from other parts of the organization complement the recovery and restoration plan
- o Communicating to the organization the importance of meeting its management requirements in order to comply with its Recovery and Restoration policies?

SUMMARY

All organizations are subject to incidents and disruptions of operations. Disruptions can be the result of terrorist or cyber-attack, natural disasters such as hurricanes, earthquakes, or floods, or internal occurrences such as fires, utility outages, hacking, or HAZMAT spills. Managers and auditors must develop and refine the ability of organizations to react to emergencies, mitigate them, and initiate restorations until normal operations are fully resumed – all while protecting the welfare and safety of their personnel and community. All phases of Disaster Planning must:

- Focus not only on mitigating the immediate effects of disasters, but on increasing resistance to future disasters.
- Have an "end state" in mind, which is better in as many measurable respects as possible, than the organization's condition prior to disaster occurrence. That is, a new "normal".
- Be linked to the planning of the community, and the goals of both should be the same.

A viable Recovery strategy (again, planned from the beginning) can be sub-divided into <u>overlapping</u> phases: Immediate Aftermath; Restoration of major services; Reconstruction and Replacement.

Managing (and auditing) Restoration seeks, as a goal, going beyond the status quo and using an unsolicited opportunity to measurably improve the structure, robustness, and sustainability of the (ultimately) restored organization; likewise, the community and the lives of the stakeholders.

CHAPTER FOURTEEN

Auditing Computer-Based Information Security – Gain Control and Keep it

> *We remain incredibly uneducated, unstructured,*
> *and vulnerable, when it comes to threats to*
> *the security of our information systems.*

DoD and, for that matter, every one of us, is in danger of physical or cyber-attack, because we remain incredibly uneducated, unstructured, and vulnerable, when it comes to threats to our security. DoD must *harden* and enforce its contracts – at their creation and fully throughout their life cycles. Our organizational security must be upgraded profoundly and continuously, through a robust program of internal and outside information security audits.

An "audit" is a systematic, independent, and documented process for obtaining evidence and evaluating it objectively, in order to determine the extent to which audit criteria have been fulfilled. *Information systems auditing* is the process of collecting and evaluating evidence to determine whether or not a computer system safeguards assets and resources, maintains data integrity, allows organizational goals to be achieved effectively, and uses resources efficiently. More on this in the sections that follow.

A.   INFORMATION CONTROL

> *"Information is the only weapon that can be in more than one place at the same time."*
> **Somebody smart**
>
> *"No good decision can come from bad data."*
> *Me*

DoD information systems process data and provide decision-making information – in the office, the laboratory, and the battlespace. Because of the focus and determination of those aggressors who would do us harm, it is vital that our information security be under the tightest, most rigorous control possible. Control also means compliance with legal, statutory, and other regulatory security requirements, security management objectives, delivery of secure products, and security throughout the supply chain.

Loss (or ineffective) control of computer information systems control can result in:

- Destruction, theft, or modification of resources
- Privacy violations
- Disruption of operations
- Physical harm to personnel.

Data is a critical resource, necessary for virtually all of DoD's missions and operations in an ever-changing environment. Lost or corrupted data, or correct data in the hands of the aggressor, can lead to loss of mission and loss of life. Decisions made as the result of bad data can be disastrous.

B.   AUDIT OBJECTIVES

In his seminal book *Information Systems Control and Audit*, University of Queensland Professor Ron Weber cites four major objectives of information systems auditing, as follows.

1. Safeguarding of resources

"Resources" are hardware, software, facilities, people, data files, system documentation and integrators, and supplies. These can be destroyed maliciously, stolen or destroyed, and/or used for unauthorized purposes. They may be concentrated in a limited number of locations; in some cases, one single disk. Physically safeguarding these personnel, spaces, and equipment is both basic and essential to an organization's security management system.

2. Improved data integrity

"Data integrity" is a condition or state implying that data has completeness, soundness, purity, and veracity. If data integrity is not (or no longer) maintained, the command, program, or mission no longer has a true and accurate representation of itself or its operations. Resultant is loss of mission effectiveness or program control. Data integrity, or the loss thereof is often described in terms of its impact on decision-making effectiveness, information sharing, and its value to opposing forces.

3. Improved system effectiveness

Auditing and evaluating system effectiveness require that auditors know exactly the objectives of the systems. The information gathered and processed must satisfy the collection and decision-making objectives for which it is being managed. For this reason, auditing must take place starting at the design stages, at implementation, and repeatedly, to ensure goals are being met and opportunities for improvement are identified.

4. Improved system efficiency

System *effectiveness*, as described above, is measured using a variety of metrics. System *efficiency* means that the system is using minimal resources to reach the required level of effectiveness.

C. AUDIT MANAGEMENT

> *"Things refuse to be mismanaged for long" - Ralph Waldo Emerson*

I am not in the habit of quoting Emerson. However, I can't help but agree with this statement.

Years ago, one of my many and often-frustrated (by me) mentors had a sign over his desk which read: *"Expect What You Inspect."* That meant (as he patiently explained): (1) that if you check on something routinely, before long you will be happy with what you see; (2) if you hardly ever check, you will not be happy, and will be forced to look at it and to fix it; and (3) that if you inspect frequently, then the area not only functions well, but continues to improve.

Looking critically at internal functions and processes and comparing findings with approved standards is the basis of the audit. An organization can audit itself, or hire an independent auditor/consultant, or a combination of both. As a result, internal (self) and external (e.g., by a registrar) audits give organizations comprehensive self-sustaining evaluation and improvement capability.

Figure 14-1 describes an effective information security management strategy for both internal and external audits.

Figure 14-1 Conducting and managing information security audits

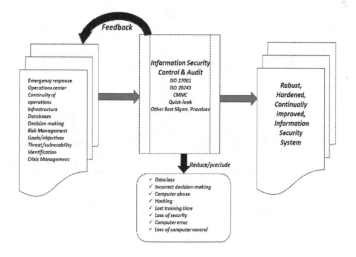

Organizations don't always do all the work required for effective audits, nor do they adequately qualify internal auditors. As a result, audits tend to be sporadic, biased, and perfunctory. More important, critical findings of the type discussed herein, may not be uncovered, and corrective actions not initiated.

Instead of executing a meaningful measure of organization security and effectiveness, unqualified or unmotivated auditors only waste time, annoy busy people, and turn off top management to the potential benefits of internal auditing.

DoD contracts are only now starting to require auditing to international standards, but thus far only in a superficial "check this block" manner. It is up to program managers not only to demand these standards in their contracts, but to make sure they are scrupulously implemented. And audited. The good news is that program managers can start immediately, by auditing their programs on their own, in accordance with the guidance provided herein and readily available off the internet. Why wait?

I have written previously for DAU (and for many years before that) about the potential *value-add* of structured information systems security management standards like ISO 27000 and ISO 20243 (Parts 1 and 2). I have audited both public and private sector organizations to these standards with very substantial results.

Table 14-1 lists three proven, readily-available, and high value, international standards for auditing information systems security. They are all available on the internet for immediate download. When implemented, the standards can measurably upgrade and continuously improve the security of any DoD information system, contract, program, or mission.

Table 14-1 Three readily available International Standards for auditing and managing Information Security

Designation	Title	Self-Audit	Certification	Available now on the net
ISO 27001-2013	Information Systems Security Management	X	X	X
ISO 20243-1 (Pts 1 & 2)	Open Trusted Technology Provider Standard (O-TTPS)	X	X	X
CMMC	Cybersecurity Maturity Model Certification	X	X	X

The International Organization for Standardization (ISO) developed *ISO 27000* to provide the requirements for establishing, implementing, maintaining, and continually improving an information security management system within an organization.

ISO 20243:2018: *The Open Trusted Technology Provide Standard (O-TTPS)* provides guidelines, recommendations, and requirements against maliciously tainted and counterfeit products in commercial off-the-shelf (COTS) information and communication technology (ICT) product lifecycles.

D.   ENTER CMMC

Now, I want to introduce Cybersecurity Maturity Model Certification, or "CMMC". Auditing a program or organization for CMMC compliance means reviewing existing policies and network diagrams, and conducting scoping interviews to examine how controlled information flows into, within, and from an organization. At the same time, a CMMC audit assesses the *maturity* of those controls (e.g., how strong they are and how equal to future tasks and challenges). The information gained from the audit creates, revises, and continuously improves an organization's CMMC System Security Plan.

The guidance in the CMMC standard can be (at times) cumbersome and repetitive. However, it is better to start with too much guidance and tailor it to what you need, rather than to have too little guidance and overlook the security of a critical process or sub-process. You can develop a checklist tailored to the mission, and, in doing so, make an arguably problematic requirements document it to an effective management tool.

Figure 14-2 is a small section of (what can become) a giant CMMC checklist, which I developed on an EXCEL spreadsheet, and made into a combination checklist and "stoplight chart". Readers are welcome to contact me for the complete spreadsheet.

The origin, necessity, and legitimacy of CMMC is questionable, as is its actual contribution to organizational security. Suffice it to say that, in my opinion, it adds nothing to an effective organizational security program, especially one created in the structure of ISO 27000 and ISO 28000. It is my hope that, by the time this book is published, CMMC has been either greatly reduced in scope, incorporated into ISO 27000, or cancelled.

Figure 14-2 A "completed" section of a CMMC checklist/stoplight chart

3.3.7 Provide a capability that compares and synchronizes internal system clocks to generate time stamps for audit records.			
Assessed	**Where to Look:**	**Assessment**	**Comment**
12-Dec	• audit and accountabilitypolicy		Update
12-Dec	• procedures addressing time stamp generation information		
12-Dec	• system design documentation		Corect ASAP
12-Dec	• information system configuration settings and associated documentation		Revise
12-Dec	• information system audit records		
12-Dec	• other relevant documents or records		
	Who to Talk to:		
12-Dec	• employees with information security responsibilities		
12-Dec	• system/network administrators		Re-train
12-Dec	• systemdevelopers		
	Perform Test On:		
12-Dec	• automated mechanisms implementing time stamp generation		Test again
12-Dec	automated mechanisms implementing internal information system sclock synchronization		Reclibrate

The colored-in boxes make for an efficient audit debriefing vehicle. Additional columns with headings such as "Objective Number," "Assigned," and/or "Completion Date" may be added, in order to turn the audit report quickly into an *actionable* plan of action & milestones, or POA&M.

5. "QUICK-LOOKS" (A much better idea, again)

Quick-looks (shown in table 14-2) are immediate, high pay-back, self-audits that forward-thinking program and security managers can use on a daily basis, to reduce the vulnerability and attractiveness of their facilities to physical or cyber-attack.

Table14- 2 A simple quick-look checklist

Designation	Quick-look	Date	SAT/ UNSAT	Remarks
I-1	Intrusion Detection Systems			
I-2	Fences, Security lighting, natural barriers			
I-3	CCTV			
I-4	Computer backup systems; firewalls			
I-5	Roof and ventilator duct accessibility			
I-6	Construction materials/thickness requirements			
I-7	Roads and alleys			
I-8	Parking areas			
I-9	Locks, doors and access control			
I-10	Identification management			
I-11	Utilities (including uninterruptible power systems)			
I-12	Safes, desks, file cabinets. Controlled/exclusion areas			
I-13	Hazmat generation and management			
I-14	Vehicle surveillance/security			
I-15	Proximity of emergency services			
I-16	Mail and package processing			

Prepared/Date _____

Reviewed/Date_____

Make a checklist like table 14-2 for your organization and fill it in by the end of the week. You'll be glad you did.

SUMMARY

DoD must *harden* and enforce its contracts – at their creation and throughout their life cycles. Instead of executing a meaningful measure of organization security and effectiveness, unqualified or unmotivated auditors only waste time, annoy busy people, and turn off top management to the potential benefits of internal auditing.

Everything program managers need for robust, cradle-to-grave; information systems security management is available *right now* on the internet. It remains only for them to download, tailor, and implement; and to make the standards their own.

Developing a real information security strategy, using the standards and checklists immediately available on the net, and taking action on your findings will improve the security posture of your program or operation – immediately and continuously; potentially saving a program, mission, and who knows what else. The success of Information Security in DoD is the result of the corrective and preventive actions that DoD Management takes as the result of audits and their findings.

DoD needs to make Information Security Management part of every program, organization, and mission, and then approach it like any other:

- Establish open communication and feedback loops;
- Establish policies and procedures; conduct gap analyses and risk assessments;
- Implement processes;
- Identify corrective and preventive actions, lessons learned and training requirements;
- Establish a mindset of continuous improvement; and
- Audit, audit, audit.

APPENDIX

Appendix I – Business Continuity Management
Appendix II – Information Security Management
Appendix III – Supply Chain Security Management

APPENDIX I – BUSINESS CONTINUITY MANAGEMENT

A. General Operations

Number	Item	Yes	No	N.A.
1	Control of access to the facility			
2	OPs available as needed			
3	Risk assessments developed for different threats, vulnerabilities, criticalities, and courses of action			
4	Car/truck bomb defenses developed/understood			
5	Perimeters established for all nodes a. Security forces posted b. Sensors in place/tested			
6	Emergency evacuation procedures developed/understood			
7	Control of locks/keys established			
8	Alarms/duress codes in use			
9	Primary and alternate communications established with all stations			
10	Weather predictions known and considered			
11	Stowaway searches conducted			
12	Threat assessment conducted			
13	Coordination with law enforcement conducted			

Number	Item	Yes	No	N.A.
14	Area cleared of potential targets/ hiding places as practicable			
15	Driver credentials verified			
16	Unnecessary porous/flammable materials removed from work areas as practicable			
17	Emergency roadblocks/barricades available or positioned			
18	Vehicle passes distributed			
19	Cargo not left unattended/unguarded			
20	Threat condition known throughout facility			
21	Container security maintained (e.g., locks, seals)			
22	Personal Protective Equipment available on site			
23	Decontamination/remediation material available on site			
24	Safe/secure areas designated			
25	Restricted areas designated			
26	In-transit cargo/product visibility maintained			
27	Safety training conducted			
28	Human factors weaknesses/problem areas identified			
29	Attack countermeasures prioritized			
30	Procedures for auditing security plans developed			

A. Tactical Operations Center (TOC) – Physical Plant or Facility

Number	Item	Yes	No	N.A.
1	Operating Procedures (OPs) developed			
2	Restricted areas designated			
3	Emergency response plans developed, including plans for maintaining critical port operations			
4	Emergency response procedures defined			
5	All port/area interfaces available			
6	Personal Protective Equipment on-site and ready			
7	Reporting procedures established/ in-progress			
8	Primary and secondary communications established			
9	All alarms tested/operational			
10	Training conducted			
11	Restricted areas defined			
12	Safe areas defined			
13	All facilities in the area alerted to the situation			
14	Alternate routes selected			
15	All positions manned			
16	All detectors networked a. Tested b. Operational			
17	Situational awareness maintained – all stations			
18	Risk assessments made			
19	Threat assessments/weather forecasts updated			
20	Ready for limited operations			
21	Ready for unrestricted operations			

B. Tactical Operations Center – On Scene Decision Making

Number	Item	Yes	No	N.A.
1	All systems installed and working			
2	TOC can be alerted by automatic alarms/detectors			
3	Operators trained and familiar with systems			
4	All applicable data loaded a. Intelligence b. Weather			
5	Key assets and vulnerabilities defined a. Piers/loading docks b. Cranes/vehicles c. MHE d. Collective protection systems e. Staging areas f. Primary roads g. Rail lines h. Port control tower i. TOC j. Exit gates k. Supporting buildings l. Pager alert warning systems m. Flashing lights			
6	Situational awareness maintained			
7	Ability to identify options and develop courses of action			
8	Primary and secondary communications established			
9	Risk assessments conducted; hazards identified and prioritized			
10	Coordination with all nodes and command posts			
11	Alternate TOC designated			

Number	Item	Yes	No	N.A.
12	Succession of command established			
13	Self-synchronization based on shared organizational monitoring			
14	Medical interface established a. Data transfer established			
15	Latest intelligence received (Time:_____)			
16	Communications with higher authority established			

C. Site Hardening – Preparing for the worst

Number	Item	Yes	No	N.A.
1	Control of access to the facility			
2	Operating Procedures created and available			
3	Risk assessments created for different threats, vulnerabilities, criticalities and courses of action			
4	Car/truck bomb defense a. Perimeter established b. Barriers in place			
5	Sensors in place; tested			
6	Communication established with all stations a. Primary_____ b. Secondary_____			
7	Emergency evacuations established			
8	Control of locks/keys established			
9	Alarms/duress codes in use			
10	Weather predictions known and considered			
11	Threat assessment last conducted_____			
12	Coordination with local authorities established			
13	Area cleared of potential targets/ hiding places			
14	Unnecessary flammable/porous materials removed from the area, as practicable			
15	Verification of driver credentials established			
16	Stowaway searches conducted			

Number	Item	Yes	No	N.A.
17	Emergency roadblocks positioned			
18	Perimeter fencing checked; integrity confirmed			
19	Vehicle passes provided			
20	Threat condition known throughout area			
21	Personal Protective Equipment available on site			
22	Container security maintained			
23	Decontamination material available on-site			
24	Safe/secure areas designated			
25	Restricted areas designated			
26	Cargo in-transit visibility maintained			
27	Alarms tested/audible			
28	Lighting adequate			
29	Land/waterborne security maintained along perimeters			
30	Automatic intrusion devices installed/ operational			
31	Barriers effective			
32	Training conducted			
33	Human factors weaknesses identified			
34	Procedures for auditing security plans developed			

APPENDIX II – INFORMATION SECURITY MANAGEMENT

Reference (and numbering): ISO 27000

4.1 General requirements

☐ Is an Information Security Management System maintained for: ensuring that products conform to requirements?

☐ Is the Information Security Management System properly documented?

☐ Does the organization:

  ○ Identify processes needed for the ISMS
  ○ Determine process sequence and interaction
  ○ Determine the criteria and methods necessary to ensure effective operation and control of processes
  ○ Ensure resource and information necessary to support operation and monitoring of the processes
  ○ Monitor, measure, and analyze processes
  ○ Implement actions necessary to achieve the planned results and continual improvement of these processes?

☐ Are the processes managed by the organization in accordance with the International Standard?

4.2 Documentation requirements

4.2.1 General

- ☐ Does Information Security Management System documentation include documented statements of quality policies and quality objectives?
- ☐ Does documentation include documentation needed to ensure the effective planning, operation, and control of the processes?
- ☐ Are quality policies accumulated in a quality manual?
- ☐ Are documentation procedures in accordance with this International Standard?

4.2.2 Information Security & Risk Management Manual

- ☐ Is the Information Security & Risk Management Manual a controlled document?
- ☐ Does the quality manual include the following:

  - ○ The scope of the Information Security Management System, including details of and justification for any exclusions?
  - ○ The organization's type and size
  - ○ The complexity and interaction of the organization's processes
  - ○ The competence of the organization's personnel
  - ○ Identification of quality controls
  - ○ Production compatibility
  - ○ Updating testing procedures
  - ○ Identification of measurement requirements
  - ○ Clarification of process and product requirements, and
  - ○ Preparation of quality records?
  - ○ A description of the interaction between the processes of the Information Security Management System?

☐ Does the organization measure, monitor, and analyze the processes established, and implement actions to ensure continuous improvement?

4.2.3 Control of documents

☐ Is there a documented procedure established to define the controls needed to:

- ○ Approve documents for adequacy prior to issue
- ○ Review and update as necessary and re-approve documents
- ○ Ensure that changes and the current revision status of documents are identified
- ○ Ensure that relevant versions of applicable documents are available at points of use
- ○ Ensure that documents remain legible and identifiable
- ○ Ensure that documents of external origin are identified and their distribution controlled
- ○ Prevent the unintended use of obsolete documents, and to apply suitable identification to them if they are retained for any purpose?

☐ Are design- and quality-related documents controlled?
☐ Are documents reviewed and approved by authorized personnel?
☐ Are quality documents available to appropriate parties?
☐ Are obsolete documents removed from use?
☐ Is there an approved distribution list for documents?
☐ Are changes to documents reviewed and approved by the same personnel initiating the documents?
☐ Are changes to designs and documents properly reviewed?
☐ Are changes identified on engineering drawings?
☐ Is there a master list for controlling documents?
☐ Are documents reissued after changes have been made?

4.2.4 Control of records

- ☐ Are records established and maintained to provide evidence of conformity to requirements and of the effective operation of the Information Security Management System?
- ☐ Do records remain legible, readily identifiable, and retrievable?
- ☐ Is there a documented procedure established to define the controls needed for the identification, storage, protection, retrieval, retention time, and disposition of records?
- ☐ Do records provide confidence that processes and resulting products conform?
- ☐ Are results of reviews and follow-up actions recorded?
- ☐ Do records indicate that reviews are conducted at suitable stages of design, development, and follow-up?
- ☐ Are the results of changes, verifications recorded?
- ☐ Are the results of subcontractor evaluations recorded?
- ☐ Are the results of calibrations recorded?
- ☐ Are there procedures for identifying, collecting, controlling, and storing quality records?
- ☐ Are quality documents and records accurate and current?
- ☐ Are the records of subcontractors and subcontractors' subcontractors accurate and current?
- ☐ Are quality records accessible?
- ☐ Are quality records retained for a sufficient amount of time?
- ☐ Are quality records available to the customer and other interested parties?

5.0 MANAGEMENT RESPONSIBILITY

5.1 Management commitment

- ☐ Is top management actively involved in the Information Security Management System?
- ☐ Are quality policies, objectives, and plans developed?
- ☐ Is a Risk Assessment/Risk Management procedure developed?

□ Does quality planning include the following:

　　○ Information Security Management System processes
　　○ Necessary resources?

5.2 Resource Management

Has Management determine the resources it needs to:

□ Establish, implement, monitor, review, maintain, and improve the ISMS;

□ Ensure that information security procedures support the business requirements;

□ Identify and address legal and regulatory requirements and contractual security obligations;

□ Maintain adequate security by correct application of all implemented controls;

□ Carry out reviews when necessary, and to react appropriately to the results of those reviews; and

Where required, improve the effectiveness of the ISMS?
Does top management ensure that customer security requirements are determined and are met with the aim of enhancing customer satisfaction?

5.2.2 Training, Awareness, and Competence

□ Are training needs and competencies identified?
□ Are training resources adequate for the internal training needs?
□ Are all personnel trained in quality technologies?
□ Are training records maintained?
□ Do training records include personnel:

　　○ Education
　　○ Experience
　　○ Training
　　○ Qualifications?

- [ ] Do personnel understand the relevance and importance of what they do and how they contribute to the achievement of quality objectives?
- [ ] Does the organization evaluate the effectiveness of the training provided?
- [ ] Does the organization define "competency" and how personnel can demonstrate competency within the Information Security Management System?

5.5.2 Security Officer

- [ ] Has a Security Officer(s) been appointed?
- [ ] (Irrespective of other duties) Does the Security Officer have the authority and responsibility to promote awareness of customer requirements throughout the organization?
- [ ] Are sufficient records maintained of organization and management quality activities?

5.5.3 Internal communication

- [ ] Does communication take place between various levels and functions regarding the effectiveness of the Information Security Management System?

6 Internal ISMS Audits

- [ ] Does the organization have and Internal ISMS Audit procedure and does it:

  - Conform to the requirements of the International Standard and relevant legislation or regulations;
  - Conform to the identified information security requirements;
  - Are effectively implemented and maintained; and
  - Perform as expected?

- [ ] Are all ISMS-related processes and procedures audited at least once per year?

7 Management Review of the ISMS

7.1 General

Are management reviews scheduled at planned intervals to ensure continuing suitability, adequacy, and effectiveness?

7.2 Review input

☐ Do management reviews include:

- ○ Results of the ISMS audits and reviews;
- ○ Feedback from interested parties;
- ○ Techniques, products, or procedures, which could be used to improve the ISMS performance and effectiveness;
- ○ Status of preventive and corrective actions;
- ○ Feedback from interested parties;
- ○ Results from effectiveness measurements;
- ○ Follow-up actions from previous management reviews;
- ○ Any changes that could affect the ISMS; and
- ○ Recommendations for improvement?

7.3 Review output

☐ Do outputs from management reviews include actions relative to:

- ○ The Information Security Management System (and its processes) improvement
- ○ Product improvement (related to customer requirements)
- ○ Resource needs
- ○ Improvement in the effectiveness of the ISMS.
- ○ Update of the risk assessment and risk management plan?

☐ Are modifications of procedures and controls that affect information security, respond to internal or external events that may impact of the ISMS, including changes to:

- ○ Business requirements;
- ○ Security requirements;
- ○ Business processes affecting the existing business requirements;
- ○ Regulatory or legal requirements;
- ○ Contractual requirements; and
- ○ Levels of risk and/or criteria for accepting risks?
- ○ Resource needs.
- ○ Improvement to how the effectiveness of controls is being measured?

8 ISMS Improvement

8.1 Continual improvement

☐ Does the organization continually improve the effectiveness of the Information Security Management System through the use of:

- ○ Information security policy and objectives
- ○ Audit results
- ○ Analysis of data
- ○ Corrective and preventive actions
- ○ Management review?

8.5.2 Corrective Action

☐ Does the organization take action to eliminate the causes of nonconformities?

☐ Does a documented procedure exist to define the requirements for:

- ○ Reviewing nonconformities (including customer complaints)
- ○ Determining the causes of nonconformities
- ○ Evaluating the need for action to ensure that nonconformities do not recur
- ○ Determining and implementing the action needed
- ○ Records of the results of the action taken
- ○ Reviewing corrective action taken?

- [ ] Is the status of corrective actions reviewed during management review?

8.5.3 Preventive action

- [ ] Does the organization determine action to eliminate the causes of potential nonconformities in order to prevent their occurrence?
- [ ] Is there a documented procedure to define the requirements for:

  - ○ Determining potential nonconformities and their causes
  - ○ Evaluating the need for action to prevent occurrence of nonconformities
  - ○ Determining and implementing action needed
  - ○ Records of results of action taken
  - ○ Reviewing preventive action taken?

APPENDIX III – SUPPLY CHAIN SECURITY MANAGEMENT

Reference (and numbering): ISO 28000

ITEM 4.1 GENRAL REQUIREMENTS

☐ Has the organization established, documented, maintained, and continually improved an effective security management system for identifying security threats, assessing risks, and controlling/mitigating their consequences?

☐ Has the organization defined the scope of its security management system, including control of outsourced processes that affect the conformity with these requirements?

ITEM: 4.2 SECURITY MANAGEMENT POLICY

☐ Has top management developed a written security policy, and is it:

   ○ Consistent with other organizational policies

   ○ Providing framework for specific security objectives, targets, and programs to be produced

   ○ Consistent with the organization's overall security threat and risk management framework

   ○ Appropriate to the threats to the organization and the nature and scale of its operations

   ○ Clear in its statement of overall/broad security management objectives

   ○ Committed to compliance with current applicable legislation, regulatory and statutory requirements and with other requirements to which the organization subscribes

   ○ Visibly endorsed by top management

- Documented, implemented, and maintained
- Communicated to all relevant employees and third parties including contractors and visitors with the intent that these persons are made aware of their individual security-related obligations
- Available to stakeholders where appropriate
- Provided for review in case of acquisition or merger, or other change to the business scope, which may affect the relevance of the security management system?

ITEM 4.3: SECURITY RISK ASSESSMENT PLANNING

- ☐ Has the organization established and maintained procedures for ongoing identification and assessment of security threats and security management-related threats and risks, and the identification and implementation of necessary management control measures?
- ☐ Are threats and risk identification, assessment, and control methods appropriate to the nature and scale of the operations?
- ☐ Does the risk assessment include:

  - Physical failure threats and risks, such as functional failure, incidental damage, malicious damage or terrorist or criminal action
  - Operational threats and risks, including the control of security, human factors, and other activities that affect the organization's performance, condition, or safety
  - Natural environmental events which may render security measures and equipment ineffective
  - Factors outside of the organization's control such as failures in externally supplied equipment and services
  - Stakeholder threats and risks, such as failure to meet regulatory requirements or damaged reputation
  - Design and installation of security equipment including replacement, maintenance, etc.
  - Information and data management and communications?

- [ ] A threat to the continuity of operations?
- [ ] Are the results of these assessments considered and do they provide input into:

  - o Security management objectives and targets
  - o Security management programs
  - o The determination of requirements for the design, specification, and installation
  - o Identification of adequate resources including staffing levels
  - o Identification of training needs and skills
  - o Development of operational controls
  - o The organization's overall threat and risk management framework?

- [ ] Is the organization's methodology for risk identification and assessment:

  - o Defined with respect to its scope, nature, and timing, to ensure that it is proactive rather than reactive
  - o Include a collection of information related to security threats and risks
  - o Provide for the classification of threats and risks and identification of those that are to be avoided, eliminated, or controlled
  - o Provide for the monitoring of actions to ensure effectiveness and the timeliness of their implementation?

- [ ] Has the organization established, implemented, and maintained a procedure:

  - o To identify and have access to the applicable legal requirements and other requirements to which the organization subscribes related to its security threat and risks
  - o To determine how these requirements apply to its security threats and risks?

- [ ] Does the organization have documented security management objectives, and do they take into account:

    - Legal, statutory, and other security regulatory requirements
    - Security-related threats and risks
    - Technological and other options
    - Financial, operational, and business requirements
    - Views of appropriate stakeholders?

- [ ] Are the security objectives:

    - Consistent with the organization's commitment to continual improvement
    - Quantified (where practicable)
    - Communicated to all relevant employees and third parties, including contractors, with the intent that these persons are made aware of their personal obligations
    - Reviewed periodically to ensure that they remain relevant and consistent with the security management policy. Where necessary the security management objectives shall be amended accordingly?

- [ ] Are security management targets established, implemented, and maintained, and are they:

    - To an appropriate level of detail
    - Specific, measurable, achievable, relevant and time-based (where practicable)
    - Communicated to all relevant employees and third parties including contractors with the intent that these persons are made aware of their individual obligations
    - Reviewed periodically to ensure that they remain relevant and consistent wit the security management objectives, and amended accordingly?

☐ Are there security management programs established for achieving the organization's objectives and targets, and are they optimized and prioritized, and do they describe:

- ○ Designated authority and responsibility for achieving objectives and targets
- ○ The means and time scale by which the objectives and targets will be achieved, and are they reviewed/amended periodically to ensure that they remain effective?

ITEM 4.4: IMPLEMENTATION & OPERATION

4.4.1 Structure, authority, and responsibility for security management

☐ Has the organization established and maintained an organizational structure of roles, responsibilities, and authorities, consistent with the achievement of its security management policy, objectives, targets, and programs, and are these defined, documented, and communicated to responsible individuals?

☐ Does top management provide evidence of its commitment to development of the security management system and improving its effectiveness by:

- ○ Appointing a member of top management who, irrespective of other responsibilities is responsible for the design, maintenance, documentation and improvement of the security management system
- ○ Appointing members of management with the necessary authority to ensure that the objectives and targets are implemented
- ○ Identifying and monitoring the requirements and expectations of the organization's stakeholders and taking appropriate action to manage these expectations
- ○ Ensuring the availability of adequate resources

- o Communicating to the organization the importance of meeting its security management requirements in order to comply with its policy
- o Ensuring any security programs generated from other parts of the organization complement the security management system
- o Communicating to the organization the importance of meeting its security management requirements in order to comply with its policy
- o Ensuring security-related threats and risks are evaluated and included in organizational threat and risk assessments as appropriate
- o Ensuring the viability of the security management objectives, targets, and programs?

4.4.2 Competence, training, and awareness

☐ Does the organization ensure that personnel responsible for the design, operation, and management of security equipment and processes are suitably qualified in terms of education, training and/or experience, and has the organization established and maintained procedures for making persons working for it or on its behalf aware of:

- o The importance of compliance with the security management policy and procedures, and to the requirements of the security management system
- o Their roles and responsibilities in achieving compliance with the security management policy and procedures and with the requirements of the security management system, including emergency preparedness and response requirements
- o The potential consequences to the organization's security by departing from specified operating procedures?

4.4.3 Communication

☐ Does the organization have procedures for ensuring that pertinent security management information is communicated to and from relevant employees, contractors, and stakeholders?

☐ Is proper consideration given to the sensitivity of security-related information?

4.4.4 Documentation

☐ Has the organization established a security management documentation system that includes but is not limited to the following:

  ○ The security policy, objectives, and targets
  ○ Description of the security management system scope
  ○ Description of the main elements of the security management system and their interaction, and reference to related documents
  ○ Documents, including records, required by this International Standard
  ○ Documents including records determined by the organization to be necessary to ensure the effective planning, operation and control of processes that relate to its significant security threats and risks?

4.4.5 Document and data control

☐ Has the organization established and maintained procedures for controlling all documents, data, and required information, to ensure that:

  ○ These documents, data and information can be located and accessed only by authorized individuals
  ○ These documents, data, and information are periodically reviewed, revised as necessary, and approved for adequacy by authorized personnel

- Current versions of relevant documents, data, and information are available at all locations where operations essential to the effective functioning of the security management system are performed
- Obsolete documents, data, and information are promptly removed from all points of issue and points of use, or otherwise assured against unintended use
- Archival documents, data, and information retained for legal or knowledge preservation purposes or both are suitably identified
- These documents, data, and information are secure, and if in electronic form are adequately backed up and can be recovered?

4.4.6 Operational control

☐ Has the organization identified operations that are necessary for achieving:

- Its security management policy
- The control of activities and mitigation of threats identified as having significant risk
- Compliance with legal, statutory and other regulatory security requirements
- The security management objectives
- The delivery of its security management programs
- The required level of supply chain security?

☐ Has the organization ensured that these operations and activities are carried out under specified conditions by:

- Establishing, implementing, and maintaining documented procedures to control situations where their absence could lead to failure to achieve the operations and activities listed above

- o Evaluating any threats posed from upstream supply chain activities and applying controls to mitigate these impacts to the organization and other downstream supply chain operators
- o Establishing and maintaining the requirements for goods or services which impact on security and communicating these to suppliers and contractors?

- ☐ Where existing designs, installations, operations, etc., are revised, do the revisions include:

  - o Revised organizational structure, roles or responsibilities
  - o Revised security management policy, objectives, targets, or programs
  - o Revised processes or procedures
  - o The introduction of new infrastructure, security equipment or technology, which may include hardware and/or software
  - o The introduction of new contractors, suppliers or personnel, as appropriate?

4.4.7 Emergency preparedness, response and security recovery

- ☐ Has the organization established, implemented, and maintained appropriate plans and procedures to identify the potential for and responses to, security incidents and emergency situations, and for preventing and mitigating the likely consequences associated with them?
- ☐ Do the plans and procedures include information on the provision of maintenance of any identified, facilities or services that can be required during or after incidents or emergency situations?
- ☐ Does the organization periodically review the effectiveness of its emergency preparedness, response and security recovery plans and procedures, in particular after the occurrence of incidents or emergency situations caused by security breaches and threats, and are these procedures periodically tested (as applicable)?

4.5: CHECKING AND CORRECTIVE ACTION

☐ Security performance measurement and monitoring

☐ Has the organization established and maintained procedures to monitor and measure the performance of its security management system, and does it consider associated threats, risks, including potential deterioration of mechanisms and their consequences, and do these procedures provide for:

- o Both qualitative and quantitative measurements, appropriate to the needs of the organization
- o Monitoring the extent to which the organization's security management policy, objectives, and targets are met
- o Proactive measures of performance that monitor compliance with the security management programs, operational control criteria and applicable legislation, statutory and other security regulatory requirements
- o Reactive measures of performance to monitor security-related deteriorations, failures, incidents, non-conformances and other historical evidence of deficient security management system performance
- o Recording data and results of monitoring and measurement sufficient to facilitate subsequent corrective and preventive action analysis, and if monitoring equipment is needed are there maintenance and calibration procedures, and are records of calibration kept?

4.5.1 System evaluation

☐ Does the organization evaluate security management plans, procedures, and capabilities through periodic reviews, testing, post-incident reports, lessons learned, performance evaluations, and exercises, and are significant changes in these factors reflected immediately in the procedures?

☐ Does the organization periodically evaluate compliance with relevant legislation and regulations, industry best practices, and conformance with its own policy and objectives?

☐ Are records kept of the results of these periodic evaluations?

4.5.2 Security-related failures, incidents, non-conformance and corrective and preventive actions

☐ Has the organization established, implemented, and maintained procedures for defining responsibility and authority for:

- ○ Evaluating and initiating preventive actions to identify potential failures of security in order that they may be prevented from occurring
- ○ The investigation of security-related
- ○ Failures, including near misses and false alarms
- ○ Incidents and emergency situations
- ○ Non-conformances
- ○ Taking action to mitigate any consequences arising from such failures, incidents, and non-conformances
- ○ The initiation and completion of corrective actions
- ○ The confirmation of the effectiveness of corrective actions taken?

☐ Are all proposed corrective and preventive actions reviewed through the security threat and risk assessment process prior to implementation?

☐ Are corrective and preventive actions taken appropriate for the magnitude of the problems and commensurate with the security management-related risks and threats likely to be encountered?

4.5.3 Control of records

☐ Has the organization established and maintained records as necessary to demonstrate conformity to the requirements of its security management system and of this International Standard, and the results achieved?

- ☐ Has the organization established, implemented, and maintained procedures for the identification, storage, protection, retrieval, retention, and disposal of records?
- ☐ Are the records legible, identifiable, and traceable?
- ☐ Are electronic and digital documentation rendered tamper-proof, securely backed-up, and accessible only by authorized personnel?

4.5. 4 Audit

- ☐ Has the organization established, implemented, and maintained a security management audit program and does it ensure that audits of the security management system are carried out at planned intervals, in order to:
- ☐ Determine whether or not the security management system:

  - ○ Conforms to planned arrangements for security management including the requirements of the whole of Clause 4 of this specification
  - ○ Has been properly implemented and maintained
  - ○ Is effective in meeting the organization's security management policies and objectives
  - ○ Review the results of previous audits and the actions taken to rectify non-conformances
  - ○ Provide information on the results of audits to management
  - ○ Verify that the security equipment and personnel are appropriately deployed?

- ☐ Is the audit schedule based on the results of threat and risk assessments of the organization's activities, and the results of previous audits, and do the audit procedures cover the scope frequency, methodologies, and competencies, as well as the responsibilities and requirements for conducting audits and reporting results
- ☐ Are audits, where possible, conducted by personnel independent of those having direct responsibility for the activity being examined?

ITEM 4.6: MANAGEMENT REVIEW AND CONTINUAL IMPROVEMENT

☐ Does top management review the organization's security management system at planned intervals, to ensure its continuing suitability, adequacy, and effectiveness, and do reviews include assessing opportunities for improvement and the need for changes to the security management system, including security policy and security objectives and threats and risks. Records of the management reviews shall be retained.

☐ Do inputs to management reviews include:

○ Results of audits and evaluations of compliance with legal requirements and with other requirements to which the organization subscribes

○ Communication from external interested parties, including complaints

○ The security performance of the organization

○ The extent to which objectives and targets have been met

○ Status of corrective and preventive actions

○ Follow-up actions from previous management reviews

○ Changing circumstances, including developments in legal and other requirements related to its security aspects

○ Recommendations for improvement?

☐ Do outputs from management reviews include any decisions and actions related to possible changes to security policy, objectives, targets, and other elements of the security management system, consistent with the commitment to continual improvement?

APPENDIX IV - GLOSSARY

Organizational Security Management Systems routinely use the following definitions:[29]

Asset
Anything that has value to the organization

Audit
A systematic, independent, and documented process for obtaining quantifiable evidence, and evaluating it objectively to determine the extent to which the Integrated Management System (IMS) audit criteria are being fulfilled. The audit can be internal (i.e., by qualified personnel) or external (i.e., by qualified personnel from outside the organization).

Auditor
Qualified, unbiased person (inside or outside the organization) with the competence to conduct an audit

Audit Team
A group of experienced employees, nominated by the SMT, who annually review the processes within OTC, IT, Organizational Development, the IMS, and other areas as needed. Audit reports are submitted to the Risk & Compliance Manager.

Availability
The property of being accessible and usable upon demand by an authorized entity

---

[29] *Quotation marks on this page denote direct quotations from an ISO Standard.*

Confidentiality
The property that information is not made available or disclosed to
unauthorized individuals, entities, or processes

Continual Improvement
Recurring mindset and processes for enhancing the Integrated Management
System, leading to a better and more effective organization. This
includes improvements in overall performance consistent with the
organization's quality, environmental, and security management
policies.

Contaminant
A foreign or unwanted material that enters and harms the environment in
a measurable way

Corrective action
An action taken to ensure a proven nonconformity does not re-occur

Cost
The amount of resources needed to achieve a particular objective

Cost analysis
Estimate of the resources that to be expended to achieve a particular
objective

Cost/benefit analysis
A method of providing top management with quantitative data for
informed decision making

Cost avoidance
The result, expressed in dollars and cents, of changing an operation to
make it more efficient

Customer
An "organization or person that receives a product" and may include
clients, purchasers, partners, stakeholders, or any other party having a
quality related relationship with you and your organization.

Document

Information and its supporting medium; documents can be paper, magnetic, electronic or optical computer disc, photograph or master sample, or a combination thereof. "Information and its supporting medium"; the medium can be paper, magnetic, electronic or optical computer disk, photograph or master sample, or a combination thereof.

Downstream

Refers to the actions, processes and movements of the cargo in the supply chain that occur after the cargo leaves the direct operational control of the organization, including but not limited to insurance, finance, data management, and the packing, storing and transferring of cargo

Energy Conservation

The optimum use of all leadership and management skills, plus all available technologies to protect the environment, reduce operating costs, and enhance competitiveness

Environment

Surroundings in which an organization operates, including air, water, land, natural resources, terrain, flora, fauna, humans, surrounding communities, and their interrelations. Surroundings in this context extend from within an organization to the global system.

Environmental aspect

An element of an organization's activities or products or services with the potential to impact the environment. A significant environmental aspect has or can have significant environmental impact.

Environmental impact

Any change to the environment whether adverse or beneficial, wholly or partially resulting from an organization's environmental aspects.

Environmental objective

An end condition that strives to achieve, consistent with its environmental policy

Environmental performance
Measurable results of the organization's management of its environmental
    aspects

Information Security
Preservation of confidentiality, integrity and availability of information;
    in addition, other properties such as authenticity, accountability, non-
    repudiation and reliability can also be involved

Information Security Event
An identified occurrence of a system, service or network state indicating a
    possible breach of information security policy or failure of safeguards,
    or a previously unknown situation that may be security relevant

Information Security Incident
A single or a series of unwanted or unexpected information security events
    that have a significant probability of compromising business operations
    and threatening information security

Information Security Management System (ISMS)
That part of the overall management system, based on a business risk
    approach, to establish, implement, operate, monitor, review, maintain
    and improve information security. The management system includes
    organizational structure, policies, planning activities, responsibilities,
    practices, procedures, processes and resources.

Integrated Management System (IMS)
Set of interrelated elements used to establish policy and objectives and ways
    to achieve and continually improve those objectives. The IMS includes
    ISO 9000, ISO 14000, and ISO 28000.

Integrity
The property of safeguarding the accuracy and completeness of assets

Interested Party
Person or group concerned with or affected by the environmental
    performance of an organization.

Internal Audit/Review

Systematic, independent and documented process for obtaining audit evidence and evaluating it objectively to determine the extent to which the environmental management system audit criteria set by the organization are fulfilled

Internal Audit/Review

Systematic, independent and documented process for obtaining audit evidence and evaluating it objectively to determine the extent to which the environmental management system audit criteria set by the organization are fulfilled

KPI's

Key Performance Indicators are measurable, replicable, and "auditable" metrics that Management can use to continuously assess its performance

Nonconformity

Non-fulfilment of a requirement

Organization

Company, corporation, firm, enterprise, authority or institution, or part or combination thereof, whether incorporated or not, public or private, that has its own functions and administration.

Preventive action

An action taken before an error actually occurs so as to prevent a failure from occurring.

Pollutant

A chemical, particulate, or refuse material that impairs the purity of water, air, or soil

Pollution

The destruction or impairment of a natural environment's purity by contaminants

Pollution Prevention

Use of processes, practices, techniques, materials, products, services or energy to avoid, reduce or control (separately or in combination) the creation, emission or discharge of any type of pollutant or waste, in order to reduce adverse environmental impacts. Pollution prevention can include source reduction or elimination, process, product or service changes, efficient use of resources, material and energy substitution reuse, recovery, recycling, reclamation and treatment.

Procedure

Documented and specified method or practice, in which to carry out an activity or a process

Product

The "result of a process" and may include any services or advice, provided to a client as well as physical goods.

Process

A "set of interrelated or interacting activities that transforms inputs into outputs." In simple terms, what you do to get something.

Record

A "document stating the results achieved or providing evidence of activities performed". It may be retained electronically or on paper

Residual risk

The risk remaining after risk treatment

Risk

The chance of injury, damage, or loss; risks cannot be avoided entirely, but can be identified and (to varying degrees) reduced or mitigated.

Risk acceptance

A decision to accept a risk

Risk analysis

Systematic use of information to identify risk, assign consistent numerical values, and to predict the impact of the risk on the mission and operations of

Risk assessment

The overall process of risk analysis and risk evaluation

Risk evaluation process of comparing the estimated risk against given risk criteria to determine the significance of the risk

Risk management means the coordinated activities to track, prioritize, mitigate, or eliminate risk to the missions and operations

Risk treatment

The process of selection and implementation of measures to modify risk

Service Realization

Delivery of services that meet all customer, and regulatory requirements

Security

Resistance to intentional, unauthorized act(s) designed to cause harm or damage to, or by, the supply chain

Security management

Systematic and coordinated activities and practices through which an organization optimally manages its risks and the associated potential threats and impacts therefrom

Security management objective

Specific outcome or achievement required of security in order to meet the security management policy. It is essential that such outcomes are linked either directly or indirectly to providing the products, supply or services delivered by the total business to its customers or end users.

Security management policy

Overall intentions and direction of an organization, related to the security and the framework for the control of security-related processes and activities that are derived from and consistent with the organization's policy and regulatory requirements

Security management programs

Means by which a security management objective is achieved

Security management target

Specific level of performance required to achieve a security management objective

Stakeholder

Person or entity having a vested interest in the organization's performance, success or the impact of its activities; examples include customers, shareholders, financiers, insurers, regulators, statutory bodies, employees, contractors, suppliers, labor organizations, or society.

Statement of Applicability

Documented statement describing the control objectives that are relevant and applicable to the Organization's ISMS.

Supplier

An "organization or person that provides a product". A supplier can be internal or external to the Organization. In a contractual situation a supplier may be referred to as a contractor.

ABOUT THE AUTHOR

Eugene A. (Gene) Razzetti retired from the U.S. Navy as a Captain in 1992, a Vietnam Veteran and having had two at-sea and two major shore commands. Since then, he has been an independent management consultant, project manager, and ISO auditor. He became an adjunct military analyst with the Center for Naval Analyses after September 11, 2001. He has authored six management books, co-authored MVO 8000, a Corporate Responsibility Management Standard, and numerous journal articles related to management systems and the Department of Defense.

He has served on boards and committees dealing with ethics and professionalism in the practice of management consulting. He is a senior member of the American Society for Quality (ASQ) and assisted the Government of Guatemala with markedly heightening the security posture of its two principal commercial port facilities.

He can be reached at www.corprespmgmt.com or generazz@aol.com. Other books by Gene Razzetti:

1. *The Executive's Guide to Corporate Responsibility Management and MVO 8000 (2ⁿᵈ Ed)*
2. *Fixes That Last – The Executive's Guide to Fix It or Lose It Management (2ⁿᵈ Ed)*
3. *The Executive's Guide to Internal Auditing*
4. *The Executive's Guide to Creating and Implementing an Integrated Management System*
5. *Make It Work or Make It Go Away – A Handbook for DoD Program Managers*

Printed in the United States
by Baker & Taylor Publisher Services